GAY

GAY

WHAT YOU

SHOULD KNOW

ABOUT

HOMOSEXUALITY

MORTON HUNT

FARRAR / STRAUS / GIROUX

NEW YORK

ACKNOWLEDGMENTS

I owe thanks to a number of people and organizations for providing me with information for this book.

I am particularly grateful to the Institute for Sex Research at Indiana University, and especially to staff members Dr. Alan P. Bell and Dr. Martin S. Weinberg, for directing me to up-to-date survey materials and other basic information. The National Institute of Mental Health, of the Department of Health, Education and Welfare, was most generous in providing me with abstracts of all articles on homosexuality published within the past few years. Estella Jernigan of "Playboy Forum" of *Playboy* magazine unearthed for me innumerable articles and news clippings on the topic from recent years. The American Civil Liberties Union provided me with a résumé of laws currently in force that deal with homosexual sex acts.

Among the individual scientists and researchers who were particularly helpful I number Dr. Ralph Blair of the Homosexual Community Counseling Center in New York, Dr. Mark Freedman of the Northeast Community Mental Health Center in San Francisco, Robert C. Kolodny, M.D., of the Reproductive Biology Research Foundation, Professor John Money of Johns Hopkins University, and Dr. Marvin Siegelman of City College, City University of New York. Michael di Capua, my editor, has been more helpful than any writer has a right to expect an editor to be.

CONTENTS

GAY

———

1

THE MANY MEANINGS OF HOMOSEXUALITY

*A personal comment by the author
of this book*

I don't remember what was playing that Saturday afternoon, so many years ago, but it must have been fascinating because for a while I didn't notice what was happening. I was a boy of eleven at the movies by myself, and what was happening was that an overcoat was slowly creeping over onto my lap. The middle-aged man who had sat down next to me kept squirming around in his seat, and every time he did so his coat flopped a little further over onto my legs. Suddenly I realized that his hand, hidden under the coat, was on my thigh and was sliding slowly toward my crotch. My heart thumped wildly and I felt sick to my stomach. I jumped up, stumbled into the aisle, and rushed out of the movie house. Outside in the bright sunlight, with people walking all around, I felt safe, but it took a long while for my heart to stop pounding and the sickish feeling to go away.

When I got home, I asked two older boys in the neighborhood what it was all about. They said the man was a queer, a fairy, a pansy, a fruit, who wanted to open my pants and play with my penis. (Today they might also have said he was a fag or a faggot or a queen.)* They laughed at me for having been afraid; although such men were crazy, they said, they were total sissies, and even boys could beat them up, because fairies couldn't fight back. Later, when I told my father about it, he sounded more serious and alarmed: he said that a man who wanted to perform sexual acts with another man or a boy was a sexual pervert. Such people, he said, were dangerous, and should be locked away in prisons or mental hospitals.

I wonder how those boys in my neighborhood, or my father, would explain Dan and Sid, two friends with whom my wife and I had dinner last month. Dan and Sid run a little antique shop in a nearby village, and we often go there to buy things from them. We find them interesting and pleasant to be with, and we've spent a number of evenings with them. Dan is forty, fairly tall, and has a strong handsome face and a deep voice; Sid is younger and smaller, is boyish-looking, and has a big sunny smile. Neither one looks feminine, but from little things they said, and tiny clues in the way they spoke,

---

* In the back of this book, beginning on page 201, you will find a list of the special terms used by or about homosexuals, together with definitions.

we guessed long ago that they were both gay. And since they live together, we also assumed that they were lovers —that they had sex with each other, and cared about each other.

For three years, neither we nor they said anything about this. Then, last month, we invited them to dinner at our house and during the evening asked them how they had met and how long they'd been together. They realized from our questions that we knew they were gay, and lovers, and that we were open-minded about it. For a moment, they hesitated; then they started talking to us about themselves freely, and with a sense of great relief. They had met in a park fifteen years ago, they said. They were attracted to each other at once, and stayed up nearly the whole night drinking beer and talking. The next night they met again, and this time went to Dan's apartment and made love; Sid discovered that, for him, sex with Dan was far more exciting than any he had ever had with girls. In the next few weeks, Dan and Sid fell in love—they used those words without awkwardness —and told each other they wanted to spend their lives together. Sid broke his engagement to a girl and moved into Dan's apartment, and they've been together ever since. Before they left our house that night, each of them told us how good it had felt to talk honestly about their love for each other to a straight (heterosexual—that is, male-female) couple like us. And we felt pleased that they had trusted us to understand and sympathize.

The man in the movie theater was a homosexual, and so are Dan and Sid, but obviously they are very different kinds of people—and only two of the many different kinds of male and female homosexuals there are. Most people don't know this: they think that homosexuality is a single thing, when in fact it is many different things. I have spent most of my adult life studying and writing about sexual behavior and love, and I have concluded that this is the most important—but the least known—fact about homosexuality. The only thing that is true of all homosexuals is that they are sexually attracted to people of their own sex. Almost everything else that is commonly said about homosexuals is true only of some of them, and not true of many or most others.

That's one of the main reasons homosexuality is so mystifying and alarming to young people. They hear many statements about what it is and what homosexuals are like, but they also read about or hear about homosexuals who don't fit that picture. They begin to wonder whether friends, teachers, neighbors who look straight are actually homosexuals who secretly do terrible things, and whom they had better avoid. They even begin to wonder about themselves: if they ever felt any attraction to someone of the same sex, or played adolescent sex games with close friends, they fear that they themselves may be "abnormal and perverted."

For no one has taught them that homosexuality takes many forms. No one has told them that there are healthy homosexuals as well as sick ones, "square" homosexuals as well as fruity ones. No one has explained to them that few people are either completely straight or completely gay throughout their lives—and that it is quite natural for heterosexual boys and girls to go through a brief period of homosexual experimentation in their adolescent years.

No one has told them these or other important truths about homosexuality because it has long been so forbidden a subject that parents and teachers could never speak about it openly. And, in the first place, few parents and teachers really knew the truth about it. Today, for the first time in thousands of years, this is rapidly changing. Social scientists have recently been doing a good deal of research on homosexuality, and they know far more about it today than they used to. And gays themselves have been talking and writing more openly about their lives and their feelings than ever before. This book will tell you what the scientists have been learning, and what the gays have been revealing. You will discover what homosexuality is—or, more correctly—what the several kinds of homosexuality are. And you will also discover how inaccurate, or wrong, or plain silly, are most of the things that most people believe about homosexuals and homosexuality.

Nine common—but mostly erroneous— beliefs about homosexuals

Here are some of the most common statements you'll hear, or have already heard, about male and female homosexuals. Each is partly right but partly—or even mostly—wrong; each is true of some homosexuals but not true of some—or even most—others.

The Belief: You can tell a homosexual by the way he or she looks and acts. Gay men dress, walk, talk, and use their hands in a "swishy" (feminine or effeminate) way.

Gay women have short hair, deep voices, wear mannish suits, and generally act "butch" (rough-tough masculine).

The Facts: According to a 1965 study by the Institute for Sex Research at Indiana University, only about one out of every six gay men is easily recognizable as a gay; all the rest dress, walk, talk, and act like straight men. Even fewer lesbians (gay women) look or act masculine; all the rest look and act like straight women.[1]

The Belief: Homosexuals don't marry. Adult men and women who never marry are probably gay; but if a man or woman who seems a little gay is married, or ever was married, he or she must really be straight.

The Facts: Data from three recent surveys indicate that one out of every five gay men and one out of every three or four lesbians were married or had been married in the past.[2] As for people who never marry, other surveys show that only about half of them have ever had homosexual experiences.[3] And looking at it the other way around, at least 2 to 3 percent of American husbands —nearly two million of them—are bisexual, that is, have sex with other men at least once in a while, although they are married and also have sex with their wives.[4] Similarly, a small percentage of married women have sex with other women at least now and then.[5]

The Belief: Homosexuals can't "make it" (have sexual intercourse) with persons of the other sex. Gay men are

[1] *Facts, figures, or statements like these, based on published scientific studies, are followed by a number. You can look up the numbers in "Notes on Sources" to determine exactly where the information comes from.*

unable to be sexually aroused by women, or to have sexual intercourse with them. Gay women are unable to be sexually aroused by men, and few have ever had intercourse with men.

The Facts: The great majority of gay men have at least sometimes been sexually aroused by women, and half or more of all gay men have had intercourse with women.[6] Most lesbians, likewise, have sometimes been sexually excited by men, and three quarters have had intercourse with men.[7] That doesn't mean gay people like sex as well with the other sex as with the same sex, but it does mean that the popular belief is largely wrong.

The Belief: Homosexuals are oversexed. They want sex much more, and have sex far more often, than heterosexual people.

The Facts: A few gay men are very active sexually— more so than almost any straight men—but they are the exceptions. In terms of averages, surveys show that most gay men actually have somewhat less, not more, sexual activity than straight men, and most gay women have less than straight women.[8]

The Belief: Homosexuals are forever trying to seduce straights (win them over and have sex with them). Gay men are often "on the make" for good-looking straight men and especially for straight boys. Gay women are often on the make for attractive straight women and girls.

The Facts: A few homosexuals do try to seduce straights, and a very few do attempt to seduce children of the same sex. But the great majority don't; they're not attracted to people who aren't also attracted to them—and straights aren't. As for trying to lead children into having sex, this is quite rare among gays—as rare, in fact, as it is among straights.[9]

The Belief: The number of gays has increased tremendously in the last few years. The gay liberation movement—the national movement to win fair treatment for gays—has encouraged huge numbers of young people to try homosexuality, and to become converted to it.

The Facts: No research study shows, and no sex expert believes, that homosexuality has increased much, if at all, in the last thirty years. One recent survey showed no more homosexuality today than in the 1940's.[10] What *has* happened is that some homosexuals have stopped keeping it secret, and have come out in the open; we *see* far more homosexuals than we used to only because more of them make it plain to the world that they are gay.

The Belief: Homosexuals are "bitchy" (sarcastic, critical, bad-tempered). They're also touchy and extremely vain.

The Facts: These beliefs are certainly true of a good many gays; such traits of personality do seem more common among gays than among straights.[11] *But only more common—not the general rule.* There are as many *kinds* of gays as there are straights—quiet ones and noisy ones, shy ones and outgoing ones, bitchy ones and good-natured ones, touchy ones and thick-skinned ones, vain ones and plain ones.

The Belief: Homosexuals do perverted, unnatural things when they have sex with each other.

The Facts: A very few homosexuals (and a very few heterosexuals) do have perverted, unnatural tastes, such as being sexually excited by their partner's urine or feces. But the vast majority of homosexuals and heterosexuals don't. The sexual acts that most male gays and female gays perform with each other most of the time are also performed, at least sometimes, by many straight people, including married couples—especially young ones.[12] Today, most marriage counselors and psychiatrists no longer think of these as perverted or unnatural acts, and in some states the laws which used to classify these acts as unnatural have been revised, and no longer do so. (In Chapter 4, we'll consider those acts in more detail.)

The Belief: Homosexuals often feel violent and hate-filled toward each other—so much so that most murders of homosexuals are committed by other homosexuals.

The Facts: A recent study of murders of homosexuals throughout the country shows that only a minority involve homosexual killers.[13] The majority are committed by persons who believe themselves to be straight but have an unusually strong hatred of homosexuality (often because they're fighting the tendency toward it in themselves). Most often, these murderers are "queer-baiters" (teen-agers who set out in gangs to beat up gays) or "hustlers" (young men who consider themselves straight but sell their sexual services to homosexuals).

These are only a few of the partly right, but mostly wrong beliefs that most people hold about homosexuals.

There are many more; we'll come across the more important ones in other chapters.

What this means is that most people have a limited and very incomplete idea of what homosexuality is. They think of male homosexuality as a single kind of personality pattern, and a single kind of behavior; and they think the same thing about lesbianism. But modern social scientists say that this is quite wrong: there are many kinds of homosexuality, and they are as different from each other as cucumbers are from potatoes, though both are vegetables.

Dr. Alan Bell, a leading member of the Institute for Sex Research at Indiana University, sums it up perfectly when he says that we should speak of "the homosexualities"—the distinctly different kinds of experience and personality that up to now have all been lumped together under the one term "homosexuality."[14] (In the same way, there are many kinds of heterosexuality, ranging from that of prostitutes and rapists to that of poetic lovers and of loving husbands and wives.) Perhaps all this will become clearer if we now meet a handful of real people who are examples, not of homosexuality, but of the homosexualities, and see for ourselves how very different they are.

*Some examples of homosexuality in
other times and places*

Imagine, now, that we are invisible spirits, and that we can move around the world as fast as light. And that we can go back and forth in time by just wishing it. And that we can see and hear, without being seen or heard. Thus equipped, we set out to observe a few kinds of homosexuality in far places and distant times.

First we streak eastward over the Atlantic and the Mediterranean, and come down in Greece, in the city of Athens, about 2,400 years ago. We enter the handsome marble house of Callias, a well-to-do gentleman, where about a dozen dinner guests are reclining on couches, sipping wine and talking philosophy. Bearded and manly, they are all married men, but at that time wives remained home when husbands went out to dine. Now the door opens, and in comes one more guest—with his son, a handsome boy hardly in his teens, curly-haired and smooth of skin. How strange, what we see now! These mature and manly men are all acting lovesick. They stare at the boy, some of them with sad and moody expressions. Others grow talkative and clever, trying to attract his attention. Still others whisper to him in low tones, paying him compliments and praising his eyes, his hair, his skin. (Later, some of them will write him poems and love letters, and swear to be faithful if he will only love them.) The boy blushes and smiles, enjoying every minute of it—and his father is pleased and proud, and hopes his son will choose wisely in selecting one of them as his lover. But about ten years from now, when the boy is a grown man, he will stop being admired and adored; he will begin to act like a man, and will look for some beautiful boy to fall in love with—and for a good woman to be his wife, run his home, and raise his children.

Now we skip a hundred miles or so to the southwest, but stay in the same century. In a valley north of Sparta, we see two small armies fighting with bows and arrows, spears, and swords. The Spartans are attacking enemy marauders from the north—who are getting the worst of it, for the Spartans are fierce fighters who thrust, slash, rush fearlessly at the enemy. We look closely; we see that many of the Spartans are fighting side by side in pairs— tanned, muscular warriors, attacking together, defending each other, showing each other how brave and ferocious they can be. They were teacher and pupil in the art of fighting and now are partners; more than that, they are homosexual lovers. They are fellow soldiers who march together, fight together, drink and sing and pray together, and lie under the same blanket in their tent at night and make love to each other. And in this part of the world, at this time in history, no one thinks this perverted or abnormal; in fact, the armies of a number of Dorian cities are made up of pairs of homosexual lovers—not perfumed, plucked, and beautified, like the effeminate homosexuals at Attica, but the fiercest and toughest fighters of the ancient world, who believe that they are better warriors for loving each other and being inspired by each other.

Northward over the top of the world we go now, to northeastern Siberia of about a century and a half ago. We come down through the winter skies into a village of tents. The people look somewhat like Eskimos, and dress heavily in warm clothing. They are called the Chukchi, and they live by raising herds of reindeer, whose milk and meat they use for food.

It is easy to tell the men and women apart by their clothing, they way they talk, the way they behave. But now we look more closely: here, cooking dinner for her husband, is a woman dressed like the others, who talks in a high female voice and acts just like a woman—but with our magical vision we see that underneath her clothing she is a man. She is a *berdache*—one of a small number of men who, as teen-age boys, felt unable to become herdsmen and fighters, and preferred to become women. When such a boy made this decision, he became "she," plucked out "her" facial hair, put on women's clothes, lived among women and learned their skills, and became feminine and seductive and sexy. Her husband, when he chose her, was not fooled; he knew what she was, and liked it. For in his tribe—and in many Eskimo and American Indian tribes in the West—a berdache was not someone to make fun of, and the man who married a berdache was not thought of as sick or wicked or peculiar. The berdache, these peoples believed, had been turned into a man-woman by magical forces, and had magical powers—she could heal, she could foretell the future. And she could be an excellent wife, and do almost everything a wife should do, including have intercourse with her husband (he put his penis into the berdache's anus, as if it were a vagina). The only thing she couldn't do for her husband was bear him children; so he had another wife, and made love to her in the more usual man-woman way, and had children by her.

Backward we go in time to about 580 years before the birth of Jesus, and back we zoom over the top of the world, to the island of Lesbos in the Aegean Sea, east of Greece. In a courtyard, a short, swarthy, rather ugly woman in her late thirties is teaching a group of young girls to dance; this is a sort of finishing school, where she instructs them in poetry, music, and other arts. Her name is Sappho, and she is a poet. She is married and has a daughter, but what she cares about most are young women: she falls madly in love with one after another of them. She adores them, she is consumed by love, she suffers and rejoices as much as any young man ever did about a young woman, or young woman ever did about a young man. Right now, Sappho is grieving because her favorite, Atthis, is about to marry. In her mind, Sappho is composing a poem, which later she writes down. It tells how she suffers for love—the love of woman for woman, which, even today, we call *lesbian* because Sappho of Lesbos was the first one who wrote about it. It sounds much like the love of man for woman, or woman for man. Here is part of her poem:

> *When I look at you, my voice fails me;*
> *My tongue is broken. Through my body*
> *A fire runs, burning, tingling.*
> *My eyes cannot see, my ears hear a roaring noise.*
> *Sweat pours down me, I shiver and shake.*
> *I am paler than grass in autumn.*
> *I feel as if death is close upon me.*
> *I am lost in love.*

Sappho never said, in her poems, whether or not she actually made physical love to any of these girls, although people who lived in her time felt certain that she did. But her love was more than an enjoyment of their bodies; it was a special kind of infatuation, a powerful romance, a passionate friendship. She herself considered it noble: in one poem she speaks of "the glorious things we did in our youth, the many pure and beautiful things." In her day, many people agreed; it was the early Christians, much later, who called this kind of love sinful and unnatural.

Finally, we soar westward over the Mediterranean Sea to Rome and forward in time to the early part of the second century A.D. We have come here, to the imperial palace, to observe the Emperor Hadrian. He's a man well worth observing—tall and powerful in his middle age, bearded and serious, a brooding but commanding figure. And a man who has achieved marvels in his reign. When he became emperor some years ago, he gave up the policy of expanding the Roman Empire through warfare and instead adopted a policy of peace. He built or rebuilt a hundred temples, libraries, and other important structures in various parts of the empire, often designing them himself or closely directing his architects. He reformed Roman law, making it more humane toward the slaves and the common people. He studied philosophy and religion, wrote poetry, and loved whatever was beautiful (he even climbed Mount Etna once, just to see the sunrise from its peak). Yet he could lead armies in battle, cold-bloodedly execute his enemies, and make the huge government run in a businesslike fashion.

But look now: this stern, serious ruler of the civilized world turns to the young man walking by his side and smiles at him, the tender smile of someone in love. For Hadrian *is* in love with Antinoüs, a girlish, curly-haired

Greek, with full lips and a rather pouty look. Hadrian had married early but always lived on polite, distant terms with his wife. If he ever cared about anyone else, it never showed—until he met Antinoüs, and fell deeply in love. From that moment on, the youth has traveled with him everywhere—and quite openly, for in the Roman Empire homosexual love has long been quite acceptable.

A year later, however, a grieving Hadrian will make it much more than acceptable. We turn the calendar forward to see what happens. Antinoüs, while traveling in Egypt with Hadrian, drowns in the river Nile. The great Hadrian is shattered by grief and publicly "weeps like a woman," as one historian writes of him. The Roman people, respecting their mighty leader, share his sorrow and honor his love. Hadrian builds a temple where Antinoüs died and declares that the dead youth is now a god—and the Romans agree. The worship of Antinoüs spreads from Egypt to the sophisticated city of Rome itself, statues of the girlish youth set a new style in Roman art, and the love of an older man for a beautiful young one becomes more highly thought of than it has been for five hundred years.

And now we move on a century to see another emperor bringing another style of homosexuality to the city of Rome—with very different results. His name is Elagabalus, and he has become emperor at the age of fourteen. He had been a priest in the temple of the Syrian god Baal, whose cult had as its priests effeminate men and as its main idol a great black stone in the shape of a penis. Now we see Elagabalus making his ceremonial entry into Rome. He is surrounded by Syrian priests, his cheeks are painted scarlet, his eyes are made up, his arms are covered with bracelets. The Romans are more amused than annoyed; they are worldly people and not easily shocked. Yet as time passes, it seems that even the Romans can be shocked. Not by the gifts and bribes with which Elagabalus seeks to win the support of the army and the people. Not by the dinners he often gives at which gold coins and gold objects are mixed in with the food. Not when he sets up the penis-idol of Baal in the very heart of Rome, and not even when he puts his homosexual favorites in positions of great power in government. All this the Romans can put up with. But they are horrified when the young emperor dresses up as a boy prostitute and publicly speaks to a gathering of the homosexuals of the city. The Romans are scandalized when he puts on a wig and poses as a whore in a whorehouse. And they are outraged when he openly holds large homosexual orgies (sex parties) at the palace itself. The army grows mutinous, the people become restless, and finally, when Elagabalus is only eighteen, his own guards slay him, drag his body through the streets, and throw it into the Tiber River. No one mourns him, and certainly no one thinks of founding a church to worship him and what he stood for.

Some examples of homosexuality in our own time and country

We've traveled around enough in time and space; now let's look at some typical examples of homosexuality in our own country today.

Some typical examples of homosexuality? *Typical* suggests that there is a *type*, and that homosexuals are pretty much alike in most ways. The truth is not so simple: they differ from each other as much as straights do, and some kinds of homosexuals are almost the very opposite of certain other kinds. Here are a few examples.

Let's listen to three young men sitting around a coffee table and talking, in a downtown Manhattan apartment, as described by gay writer Wallace Hamilton in his book *Christopher and Gay*. No mistake about these three: they'd be the first to call themselves real "nellies" (swishy, effeminate, super-girlish). All three look the part. They all have very special hairdos, and they're wearing flowered shirts and assorted rings, bangles, and bracelets. One is even wearing heavy make-up and has a gauzy scarf draped over his shoulders. "Honey," they call each other, and "Darling," and "Mary," speaking in lisping, exaggerated feminine tones. Not schoolgirl feminine, but prostitute feminine, or promiscuous-woman feminine, for they're all used to playing a sort of female part toward other male gays and picking up strangers for "one-night stands" (they have sex with the stranger for one night, and never see him again). Bobby, the one with the scarf, is telling about a recent one-night stand: "So I'm coming up from Danny's and I see this humpy number. Oh, Miss Thing, he was hung! And I said to myself, honey, I'm going to do his buns." (This means that the stranger was well-built, especially in the crotch, and that Bobby planned to have sex with him.) Bobby struck up a conversation with the man, who claimed he was straight.

Bobby said, "I mean, Mary, you'll get *over* it!" He talked the man (he says) into coming home with him and gave him a thorough lesson in homosexual sex. "And," says Bobby with a giggle and a wiggle, "he loved every gleaming minute of it!"

Now, by way of contrast, let's look in on a gang of four teen-age toughs sitting on the steps in a poor part of a Southern city. They wear leather jackets, blue jeans, and sneakers; they smoke, spit, talk tough, punch each other around. Finally one of them says it's about time to go "fruit-hustling," it's time to "get a queer." They all agree; the weekend is coming and they need money. Fruit-hustling means standing around on any one of various corners downtown where certain adult male gays know they can be found. Such a man will approach a hustler and offer him five or ten dollars for sex. The "john" (customer) takes the hustler to a private place— his car, his apartment, or even a back alley—for a quick act of sex. It is understood by johns and hustlers that only one kind of sex act (mouth-genital contact) is being sold or allowed. It is also understood that it is the john who "does" the hustler—the hustler never touches the john or his sex organs, and this is a point of pride with him. "I just let *them* do it," a hustler will say, "I don't do anything." And because the hustler doesn't do anything, and takes money from the john, he thinks of it as a mere job, not sexual pleasure; he thinks of himself as straight. "No matter how many queers a guy goes with, if he goes for money, that don't make him queer. You're still straight." But if the homosexual john urges the hustler to "do" *him*, the hustler may fly into a rage and beat him senseless. "What does that queer think?—that *I'm* queer?"

We're in a restaurant now, in a well-known Eastern resort town. It's a gay restaurant, but there's nothing outside to alert the passerby. Straight couples occasionally come in and fail to notice, at first, that nearly all the customers at the bar and at the tables are men. Most of them are in their twenties and thirties, almost all are wearing tasteful, well-fitting sport clothes, and very few are overweight. Aside from these clues, the straights wouldn't see anything that looks or sounds particularly gay—at least, not early in the evening. Later on, after 11 P.M. or so, the music starts; then the straights would see men dancing with other men and holding each other and looking at each other—even occasionally kissing—as straight couples do. As startling as this behavior seems to most straights at first, some find it a respectable scene, once they get used to it.

A group of local roughnecks barged in here early one evening, before the dancing started; they wanted to make trouble but were disappointed when they saw nothing to insult anyone about, and stomped out again. Unfortunately, they came back later—and were able to turn the place into a shambles of overturned tables, bloodied noses, and broken glassware. But the gays gave as good as they got, and the toughs haven't been back.

Jack is a typical homosexual—at least, he represents one type of homosexual. But you'd never know it if you met him on the job or at home. He's an insurance broker, thirty-two years old, and lives with his wife and three children in a house in the suburbs. All week long at work and at home, and among their friends, he is as straight as anyone you ever saw. But Friday nights he goes off to be with "the boys" for an evening of cards—or so he tells his wife. Actually, he goes to a public bathhouse, where he signs in under a false name. It's a steam bath that is used only by male gays—and not for steam or exercise, but as a place to have sex with strangers. Jack wanders around the steam rooms, the pool, and the hallways with a towel around his waist, looking the other men over. In nearly every room, men are having sex with other men, often with others watching. Jack doesn't speak to any of them. With hardly a word he has sex with one man in the steam room, rests a while, starts in with another, then a third and a fourth. At 3 A.M. he showers and dresses, goes home, and crawls into bed next to his wife, to resume his regular life.

Is he typical? Yes, of one kind of homosexual. But so is Arnold typical, of another kind. He's a writer, and he's fiftyish, short and thickset, wears horn-rimmed glasses, and doesn't look or sound particularly gay. But for nearly his whole adult life he has lived with one man or another —there have been three, in all—and made no effort to hide the truth from his editors or family. He and his current lover have been together six years and lead a very "married" life. They have a house in the country, take turns shopping and cooking, have friends in to dinner, go to parties together. They don't swish, they don't "cruise" (go looking for strangers for instant sex), and they care deeply about each other. They do, however, have fights from time to time: Arnold is tidy, and his partner is a slob; Arnold is something of a nag, and his partner gets fed up with him now and then.

What's typical? Drop in at any "dyke" bar (a bar for female gays) and you'll see that many of the patrons belong to one or another of two fairly distinct types. One type is the "femme"—the feminine-looking girl or woman, often pretty, usually coy and flirtatious. The other is the "butch" or "bull dyke"—a girl or woman who swaggers around, talks tough, wears Levi's, boots, a leather jacket, or other items of unfeminine clothing. (If she's particularly masculine, she may even be called a "diesel dyke," because she seems tough enough to be the driver of a diesel truck.) In such a bar, as in similar gay bars for men, the strangers shuffle around, cruising—looking each other over, making contact, then going home for a one-night stand; and then goodbye.

That's typical. But Alice and Jennie are also typical. They're in their mid-thirties and both of them look like any young divorcees (which both of them are) you might see at work or in the supermarket. Jennie is the prettier of the two, but you'd never take her for a femme; Alice is a little bit stronger in manner, but you'd never take her for a butch. They've shared an apartment for over a year, and each tells her family and friends that they're roommates. Each one goes out with a man now and then to keep up appearances. But they're lovers, and hope to remain so for a long while. They keep it secret because they haven't the courage to come out with it; besides, both of them are schoolteachers, and they're afraid they'd be fired if the truth were known. So they almost never go to lesbian parties or bars. It's a lonely sort of life: their only close friends are two other couples like themselves, and a number of straight couples to whom they never hint at the truth, and who either don't suspect, or pretend that they don't.

These are only a few of the kinds of homosexuals in America today. Clearly, there are great differences among them. Some seem neurotic (emotionally sick), but some seem perfectly healthy. Many are secretive and ashamed, but some are open and unashamed. Some have only the most impersonal and ugly kinds of contact with other homosexuals; some have intimate and loving contacts with other homosexuals. Some are wholly homosexual, others have had relationships with both sexes, and still others are homosexual for a while and then become permanently heterosexual.

Therefore, no single, overall attitude or belief about homosexuality can be correct or fair-minded. To say or think anything about homosexuality that is intelligent and unbiased, you have to specify *which kind* of homosexuality you're talking about. Of course, it's simpler to have a single overall attitude or belief about the subject, but there's a name for that: ignorance. Or maybe an even better one: prejudice.

2

WHAT CAUSES HOMOSEXUALITY?

One question, many answers

If you ask half a dozen ordinary people what causes homosexuality, you'll almost certainly get several very different answers—maybe even half a dozen. That must mean that most people don't understand it, because half a dozen different explanations can't all be right, can they?

But if you ask half a dozen social scientists and doctors what causes homosexuality, you may not do any better. In the past quarter of a century, hundreds of them have been doing research on the cause of homosexuality—and the most remarkable thing about it is how many different theories they've come up with. Yet if one of their theories is right, the others can't be right, too, can they?

Before you answer that, maybe you'd like to know what the most common answers and theories are. Here are a dozen of them. The first three are offered mostly by ordinary people. The rest—except for the very last one—are the theories favored by different scientists; many ordinary people, of course, also believe in one or another of these explanations. The very last answer is given chiefly by homosexuals themselves. Which one do you think is right or most nearly right?

Seduction: Children and teen-agers turn into homosexuals because older homosexuals seduce them.

Bad example: Young people become homosexuals if they see homosexuality all around them or have homosexual friends.

Unattractiveness: If people are unattractive to persons of the other sex, they're likely to become homosexuals.

Sex segregation: People become homosexuals if they have to live in close contact with only persons of their own sex and learn to prefer them.

Heredity: Homosexuals are born that way; it's hereditary like eye color or skin color.

Congenital defect: Homosexuals are born that way, but not because of heredity; instead, something went wrong with their nervous systems while they were developing in the womb.

Hormone imbalance: Homosexuality is the result of a disorder of the endocrine glands, the glands that make the sex hormones. A gay man hasn't enough male hormones, a lesbian hasn't enough female hormones.

Wrong upbringing: People become homosexuals if they're raised to think and act like persons of the opposite sex—as when boys are made into sissies, or girls into tomboys.

Running away from it all: A homosexual male is one who can't face the challenges of being a man at work or at home. A lesbian is a female who is afraid to be a woman, wife, and mother.

Emotional sickness: Homosexuality is a kind of emotional illness caused by problems the child had with his or her parents while growing up.

Natural impulse: Homosexual desires are as natural as heterosexual desires. We'd all perform homosexual acts if our society taught us that it was all right to do so.

Taste: Homosexuality is just a matter of individual preference. Some people prefer vanilla and others prefer chocolate. It's the same with sex.

Have you made your choice? Or did you guess the truth—that there isn't any one correct answer?

The biggest problem most people have in understanding homosexuality is that they think of it as a single way of feeling and acting, and therefore look for a single way of explaining it. But as we've seen, there are a number of very different kinds of homosexuality. It doesn't make sense to think that they all have the same cause, that there is a single explanation for all of them. It makes much better sense to look for different explanations for the different kinds of homosexuality. The question to ask is: "Which of these explanations account for some kinds of homosexuality—and which kinds?" And the answer is that nearly all of them explain some kinds of homosexuality but not others—and that most homosexuality involves several of these explanations at once, several causes working together.

Now let's see which of the above theories are valid, and to what extent, and how a number of them can be right at the same time.

Seduction

Many people believe that homosexuals are as they are because, when they were young, older homosexuals seduced them. That's why, in a recent survey, three quarters of a group of average Americans said they felt that homosexuals are dangerous as teachers or youth leaders because they try to get sexually involved with young people.[15] But this isn't so. As we saw in Chapter 1, studies of sex criminals show that few homosexuals make sexual approaches to children. Furthermore, only about one out of four homosexuals in various studies claims that he or she is that way because of having been seduced by an older homosexual. Even so, in most of these cases, the child or young person was willing and did as much seducing as the older one.[16]

This means that seduction might, at most, be the cause of homosexuality in only a few cases. But probably it isn't *the* cause even in those; more likely, it is only a minor *contributing* cause, playing a part only when more important causes are at work. By itself, "child seduction is virtually powerless to start a sexual pattern," says psychologist C. A. Tripp, an expert on homosexuality. He finds that usually the "victim" was inclined toward homosexuality already.[17] The seduction only triggered off what would have developed sooner or later.

Bad example

Many people think of homosexuality as something "catching," like a contagious disease; the main cause of homosexuality, they feel, is exposure to people who have already caught it.[18] If this were true, the gay organizations and clubs which, in recent years, have come out in the open in most cities and on most college campuses would have caused a big rise in the number of homosexuals in this country. But as we have seen, there hasn't been such a rise. Most children, in their earliest years, develop heterosexual preferences, and psychologists generally feel that children who are well started toward heterosexuality aren't likely to be remade later on by the mere example of gays around them.[19] In other words, a young person who "catches" homosexuality from friends or acquaintances probably had a strong homosexual inclination in the first place; the friends and acquaintances only make it easier for the young person to acknowledge his or her homosexuality.

This account, by a male gay,[20] shows the part the so-called Bad Example actually plays:

I was gay long before I admitted my homosexuality to myself, long before I ever had sex, long before I knew what sex was. When I was ten, I played paper dolls with the girls and dug it; when I had to, I played baseball with the guys and didn't dig it. Don't get me wrong. I was not exactly a flaming faggot. I drove a tractor, plowed the fields, tossed bales of hay into the hay loft.

I went to a small liberal arts college near my home for two years. It was a parochial, superstraight middle class place, everything based on a social pecking order of fraternities and sororities. Even the lowest fraternity—a bunch of creeps—didn't want me. My gay self was showing through.

Two years later a good friend came out [that is, admitted his homosexuality]. At first I played straight; finally I admitted that I was gay too. We had been friends since we were seven years old. But it was not until we were twenty-two or twenty-three that we could deal with what brought us together.

So teen-agers and adults don't "catch" homosexuality from the example of others. The Example merely helps the homosexually inclined person to recognize and admit the truth about his or her own feelings. Somewhat like seduction, the Example does not so much *cause* homosexuality as bring it to light.

Unattractiveness

About three out of every ten Americans believe that people become homosexual because they're unattractive to persons of the opposite sex.[21] But no researcher has found any evidence to back up this belief.[22] Anyway, it doesn't make much sense. Why would gays be any more willing to accept an unattractive person as a lover than straight people would?

Yet there *is* a grain of truth in this belief. A young

man, even if he isn't ugly, may feel unattractive to girls because he thinks his looks are not manly enough. A young girl, even if she isn't ugly, may feel unattractive to men because she thinks herself not very feminine-looking. Many teen-agers have just such doubts about themselves, but most of them grow out of it. Some, though, don't grow out of it, and for good reason: they have a hidden tendency toward homosexuality which persons of the other sex don't recognize but take to be a lack of "sex appeal." Thus, unattractiveness to the other sex may be linked with homosexuality, after all—not as a *cause* of it but as a *result* of it.

Sex segregation

The theory that people become homosexuals if they are forced to live in close contact with persons of their own sex, away from persons of the other sex, has some good evidence behind it. For instance, nearly half the men in men's prisons and the women in women's prisons take part in homosexual acts with other prisoners—and this is four times as many as were involved in homosexuality before entering prison.[23] And it is well known that there is more homosexual behavior in boys' boarding schools, girls' boarding schools, and on naval vessels than in normal life.

But psychologists and sociologists say there's a great difference between a homosexual *act* and a homosexual *preference*. To take part in homosexual acts when you have no other choice isn't the same as to do so when you do have a choice, because you *prefer* them. In prison, many men and women will eventually resort to homosexual acts for relief, but this does not turn them into real homosexuals. Most of them return to heterosexuality as soon as they get out.[24] There are, of course, some true homosexuals in boarding schools, on naval vessels, and in prisons, but almost all of them were homosexual before they got there. They simply became more active, or more open, because of the special opportunities of the situation.

So while it's quite true that keeping men apart from women, or women apart from men, does cause a good deal of homosexual behavior, it rarely causes permanent homosexuality.

Heredity

About a century ago, some researchers began to think that homosexuality was hereditary, and that homosexuals couldn't do any more about it than they could about their eye color or skin color. The researchers came to this conclusion because most of the homosexuals they were able to study were in mental hospitals and had various physical and mental defects that were hereditary. It seemed possible that their homosexuality was connected with those defects—and was, itself, an inherited defect.

Possible—but not really proven. Then in 1952 Dr. Franz Kallmann, a geneticist—one who studies heredity—did find what seemed real proof. He studied a great many pairs of twins—fraternal twins, who look somewhat alike, and identical twins, who look exactly alike. Fraternal twins come from different eggs and different sperm cells, and have only about half the same chromosomes—and hence only about half the same hereditary traits. Identical twins come from a single egg, fertilized by a single sperm cell, that splits and becomes two; such twins have exactly the same set of inherited traits. If homosexuality were due to heredity, and if one of a pair of identical twins was homosexual, the other ought to be, too. But that wouldn't be nearly as true of fraternal twins. And indeed, in every pair of identical twins that Dr. Kallmann studied, if one twin was homosexual, so was the other. But if one twin of a fraternal pair was homosexual, there was only one chance in eight that the other was, too. To Dr. Kallmann, this proved that homosexuality was hereditary.[25]

But most psychologists and sexologists weren't convinced. There is another and better explanation as to why identical twins would be alike in their sexual preference: they grow up in identical environments and have essentially the same life experiences. All during childhood and adolescence, they live in the same home and spend virtually all their time together; and because they have almost identical physical and mental abilities and look exactly alike, they interact with other people, and are treated by those people, in just the same way. In short, every influence that can shape them as they develop is the same. But since fraternal twins often have very different abilities and appearances, they may have quite different experiences in growing up.

No wonder identical twins are more apt to be alike, sexually, than fraternal twins. The heredity theory would be proven only if identical twins were separated as infants and reared apart from each other—and then both grew up homosexual. But none of Dr. Kallmann's twins had been reared apart, and so his theory remains unproven—and less convincing than the environment-and-life-experience theory.

Besides, human behavior is not completely controlled by heredity in any other area, so why should it be in the area of sex? For instance, it has recently been proven that how well we score on intelligence tests is not due only to our inborn powers but is much influenced by how we have been educated and what kind of home we have grown up in. The same is true of how well we speak and write, use tools, and defend ourselves from attack. It would stand to reason, then, that sexual preference would be partly, or even largely, *learned*, shaped by experiences, rather than completely controlled by heredity.

This doesn't mean that heredity has nothing to do with homosexuality. What most social scientists now believe is that heredity gives some people a *tendency* toward homosexuality. But it is only a very general tendency, and it doesn't mean that the person will definitely become a homosexual; it only means there is a somewhat greater chance of it than usual.[26]

A boy may, for instance, be gentle and shy by nature, and this may cause his family and friends to treat him, in childhood, as if he were a sissy and were bound to grow up queer. If they treat him that way, there's a good chance he'll come to think of himself that way and grow up to be a homosexual of the obviously effeminate kind. But in a different family and neighborhood, he might grow up to be a sensitive and shy heterosexual. Even a boy whose inborn tendency is to be rough and tough can grow up to be a butch homosexual, given certain conditions and experiences in childhood.

So it seems that heredity isn't, by itself, the cause of homosexuality; it does, however, sometimes provide raw material which is more likely than usual to develop into a homosexual person. But whether that does or doesn't happen depends to a very large degree on how experience molds the raw material.

Congenital defect

An old popular belief is that homosexuality is the result of something that goes wrong with the nervous system of an otherwise healthy fetus as it is developing in the mother's womb. The child is born a physically normal male or female, but some part of its brain gives it the instincts of the other sex. A male homosexual has a "female soul in a male body"—a man outwardly, but with female instincts. A lesbian has a male soul in a female body.

Recently, biologists have performed experiments that seem to back up this rather fanciful notion. In the laboratory, they inject a pregnant guinea pig with male hormones, which reach the babies in her womb through her blood. If the injection is given at just the right time, female babies are born looking thoroughly female but grow up with male sexual instincts. They resist being mounted by male guinea pigs, but they themselves act like males and try to mount other females. In the same way, male babies can be influenced in the womb, so that although they look male, they grow up to act sexually more like females.[27]

What happens, it seems, is that the hormones upset the development of a part of the baby's brain known as the hypothalamus just as it is about to differentiate—just as it is about to develop into a male hypothalamus or into a female one. It goes the "wrong" way, and this error is permanent. Since the hypothalamus is the part of the nervous system that governs the animal's sexual instincts, the female grows up to act like a male, and vice versa.

Some people have jumped to the conclusion that something like this must happen in human beings, too. If a woman takes the wrong pills, or eats the wrong food, or has an illness while she is pregnant, perhaps the baby's developing hypothalamus differentiates incorrectly and doesn't match the baby's sex. What looks like a boy grows up feeling and acting like a girl, and vice versa. That's what some homosexuals believe, especially some of those who seek to have surgery to change their external sex organs.

But this can hardly be the cause of most, or even much, homosexuality. Human beings aren't guinea pigs, and instinct has little to do with how we behave; chiefly, we behave in ways we learn while growing up. If homosexuals had the wrong kind of hypothalamus, and if human sexual behavior were instinctive, all male gays would act like women and all female gays like men. But we have seen that this isn't so. They don't even stick to sex acts typical of the opposite sex, as we'll see in Chapter 4.

Does that mean that there's no truth to the idea that homosexuality is caused by congenital defects? Biologists and psychologists haven't nearly enough evidence to give a final answer to this question. From the evidence they do have, however, they feel that congenital defects of the hypothalamus may *help cause* many cases of homosexuality, but don't cause homosexuality by themselves. Psychologists say that the way a child is raised in its first few years has far more influence than a congenital mistake in the hypothalamus. The built-in mistake predisposes the baby to become homosexual—that is, makes homosexuality more likely than usual—but this predisposition is only a readiness to respond to certain kinds of experience. Without such experience, the baby will still grow up heterosexual.[28]

Hormone imbalance

When animals haven't enough of the right sex hormones, which are made by the endocrine glands, they lack the normal sexual impulse. As every pet owner knows, an "altered" dog—a male with his testicles removed, or a female with her ovaries removed—has no sex drive and isn't particularly male or female in general behavior. And experiments show that if an animal gets a dose of the wrong hormones, it will act like a member of the other sex: a hen given an injection of male hormones will peck other hens and try to mount them as if it were a rooster.

Many doctors used to think, therefore, that male homosexuals must not have enough male hormones and lesbians must not have enough female hormones. So when human sex hormones were first made artificially, in the 1940's, doctors tried giving them to homosexuals, thinking this would make them behave like heterosexuals. It did no such thing. Doses of male hormones only made male gays more sexually active with other male gays. Doses of female hormones didn't increase sexual activity in lesbians, but neither did the treatment change them; they remained as lesbian as ever.

Doctors concluded that it wasn't a shortage of the right hormones that caused homosexuality, and the theory was junked for many years. But in 1971 it was revived. Medical researchers at the Reproductive Biology Research Foundation in St. Louis found a highly accurate way to measure the amount of hormones in the blood. They then tested the blood of a group of homosexual men and a group of straight men, and compared the results. Three quarters of the gay men had as high a male hormone level as the straight men, but the remaining quarter of the gays had far lower levels—and these gays were the most homosexual of the whole group: they had rarely, if ever, been sexually excited by females.[29]

So it would seem that a shortage of hormones *is* connected with homosexuality, at least in some men who are thoroughly homosexual in their feelings and experiences. The doctors don't know yet why this is so. Perhaps the lack of hormones does, in some way, help cause homosexuality, but possibly it's the other way around. Possibly the emotional strain of being a homosexual upsets the endocrine glands in these men and diminishes the output of hormones. Much more research will have to be done before we have the answer.

Wrong upbringing

The novelist Merle Miller recently told why, in his opinion, he had grown up to be gay. His parents had wanted a girl, and often told him so when he was little. His mother dressed him in pink and, at a time when only girls wore long hair, kept his hair long until he was in kindergarten. He wanted to be the girl his mother had in mind, and it showed: the older boys took one look at him, his first day in school, and called him "sissy." He never had a chance to be anything else.

Stories of this sort are often told by certain gays to explain their homosexuality. An effeminate or nellie male may say that his parents—usually his mother—taught him to be girlish rather than boyish. A butch lesbian may say that her parents had wanted a boy, and taught her to be the next best thing, a tomboy.

Similarly, a male gay may say that because his father was dead, or divorced from his mother, he grew up with only a woman to model himself on. A lesbian whose mother was dead, and who was raised by her father, may say that she had the wrong kind of training for life as a woman.

But the wrong-upbringing theory seems wrong about as often as it seems right. Many male gays and lesbians weren't sissies or tomboys in childhood, most sissies and tomboys don't turn out gay, and most children of divorced parents grow up straight. So how good can the theory be?

Pretty good, at that, for it has recently been proven that a person born as a boy can be taught to think and feel like a girl and to live life that way, and vice versa.[30] A team of medical specialists at Johns Hopkins University has treated a number of children with deformed sex organs. Sometimes the only way the doctors could fix a boy's sex organs through surgery was to make them look like those of a girl. When this was the case, the doctors also had to make the child over, psychologically, into a person of the other sex. One baby boy—one of a pair of identical twins—had an accident in which his entire penis was lost. The doctors told the parents that they couldn't make a new penis, but that they could, through surgery, make a pretty good vagina. The parents agreed: the baby was operated on, renamed, and raised as a girl. From puberty on, she will take female hormone pills to make her develop breasts and to prevent the growth of a beard. She has grown up a typical girl in her behavior and her attitudes—and very different from her identical twin brother, who is in every way a typical masculine boy. In adulthood, she will undoubtedly behave very much like a typical heterosexual woman and he like a typical heterosexual man.

This still doesn't prove that wrong upbringing is ever responsible for homosexuality; it only tells us that it can cause a person to grow up behaving and feeling like someone of the opposite sex. But we've seen that a great many homosexuals don't behave or feel like persons of the opposite sex, even though they're drawn to persons of their own sex emotionally and sexually. Still, the personal statements of a number of gays do indicate that wrong upbringing probably has something to do with the homosexuality of the effeminate male, the masculine female, and the transvestite, a person (usually homosexual) who dresses, acts, and lives like someone of the other sex.

Running away from it all

Some psychoanalysts have said that their male homosexual patients feel that it's just too difficult to be a man in our society—it's hard to compete with other men at work, to be the head of a family, and to live up to a woman's sexual expectations. One way out is the "flight from masculinity," the choice of a passive, feminine personality and a way of life that is more like that of a woman than a man—at least, like that of an old-fashioned woman. And this leads to male homosexuality—at least, of the passive, effeminate kind.

In much the same way, it is sometimes said that lesbians are women who are afraid of, or dislike, the place of women in our society and in marriage. And indeed some lesbians say just such things. One of them recently told a psychiatrist that when she was a young child, it seemed to her that "to get any place in life you had to be a boy. For a time I dreamed of some miraculous change. As a child I played 'house' with the girls, and I always played the role of husband and father." As she grew up, she aimed at a business career, acted masculine, and became a butch lesbian, always picking out a soft, feminine partner.[31]

This theory does seem to explain some cases of homosexuality. But it's not enough, by itself. It doesn't explain the masculine, competitive male homosexual, or the soft, feminine lesbian. And it doesn't explain why so many other boys and girls, living in the same world as the "runaway" gays, grow up straight.

There must be a reason why being a man, or being a woman, looks worse to those who run away than it does to the majority of boys and girls. Almost certainly, it's the way a child sees masculinity or femininity at an early age—something about the child's particular family that makes being a man, or being a woman, look more frightening to that boy or that girl than it does to most others. And that's our next theory.

Emotional sickness

The theory that homosexuality is an emotional sickness that parents create in the child is probably the most widely held of all. In recent years, however, gay liberationists have fiercely attacked it, and many social scientists have come to think that it doesn't apply to all or even to most homosexuals.

But a great many straight people still find that most of the homosexual behavior they see or hear about seems definitely "sick," that it is the kind of peculiar, unusual behavior we commonly call "neurotic," or "crazy," or "screwed up." For example: the diesel dyke, dressing and acting like a male tough, and trying to disguise the female body she was born with, as if she were ashamed of it. For example: the flaming faggot, with his exaggerated make-up and his shrieks and giggles. For example: the married businessman risking his reputation and marriage for five minutes of sex with a male hustler in an alleyway.

Many gay people, too, believed in the emotional-sickness theory until recent years. Some of them even welcomed it, because it took the "blame" off them; it said that their parents had made them emotionally ill when they were innocent little children and couldn't help themselves. Here, for instance, is part of a speech by Michael, one of the male gays in Mart Crowley's play *The Boys in the Band:*

> My [mother] refused to let me grow up. She was determined to keep me a child forever and she did one helluva job . . . She made me into a girl-friend dash lover. We went to all those goddamn cornball movies together. I picked out her clothes for her and told her what to wear and she'd take me to the beauty parlor with her and we'd both get our hair bleached and a permanent and a manicure. *And Walt* [his father] *let this happen.* And she convinced me that I was a sickly child who couldn't run and play and sweat and get knocked around . . . And here I am—unequipped, undisciplined, untrained, unprepared and unable to live!

Similar statements have been made by many lesbians.

There are a number of versions of the emotional-sickness theory. Sigmund Freud, the founder of psychoanalysis, didn't call homosexuality an illness, but he did consider it the result of faulty or defective emotional development. In his view, the homosexual was a person who remained stuck at an early stage of psychological growth and never went on to the later ones.[32]

Until recently, most other psychologists and psychiatrists went further than Freud and called homosexuality an emotional sickness. Some found evidence in their patients to prove that male homosexuality was due to a pathological fear of women, while lesbianism was due to a pathological fear of men. Others, however, found evidence in their patients to prove that homosexuality was due to an excessive attachment of the boy to his mother —what we mean when we say someone is a "mama's boy" —or of the girl to her father.[33]

Whether homosexuality is due to fear of the opposite sex, or to an overattachment to the parent of the opposite sex, it's the fault of one or both parents, according to all versions of the emotional-sickness theory. Many researchers have described the various kinds of parent-child relationship that create this illness in children. Sometimes a mother is too domineering, sometimes a father is too domineering; perhaps the mother is cold and unloving, or the father is. The most common situation of all, at least in the childhood of male homosexuals, is the combination of a strong, overprotective mother and a weak, unloving, or absent father (just as Michael described it). That, at any rate, was the finding of Dr. Irving Bieber and certain other members of the Society of Medical Psychoanalysts who pooled their experiences treating male homosexual patients and published the results in 1962.[34]

But Dr. Bieber's group, and other psychotherapists who said homosexuality was an emotional sickness, based their conclusions on what they saw in their patients. Of *course* all those patients had emotional problems; that's why they came in to be treated in the first place. But what about all the other homosexuals who never felt the need to go to a psychotherapist for treatment? Who could say whether they, too, were sick or not? Could it be that their sexual preference was not part of an emotional sickness?

A psychologist named Evelyn Hooker had been pondering these very questions for some years. In 1957 she picked out a group of homosexual men who weren't patients, and who appeared to be emotionally and socially well-adjusted, and gave them psychological and personality tests. She also gave the same tests to a group of heterosexual men. Then she asked several psychologists to study the tests and see if they could tell which had been taken by homosexuals. They couldn't. The gays had much the same state of emotional health as the straights. This didn't mean that all homosexuals are emotionally healthy, for Dr. Hooker had picked healthy-seeming ones to start with. What it did mean was that not all homosexuals are emotionally sick—that homosexuality isn't *necessarily* the result of emotional illness.[35]

Since then, dozens of similar studies have been made with larger and more representative samples of gays, both male and female. Some show that gays have more emotional problems than straights; others show that most gays are about as healthy, emotionally, as most straights. Depending on which studies you choose, you can "prove" either side of the argument—that gays are sick, or that gays are well.

But if you're not out to win an argument, you can only conclude that the truth lies somewhere in between. As Dr. Judd Marmor, an authority on homosexuality, sees it, there are many healthy homosexuals, but taking them all in all, there does seem to be somewhat more emotional illness among homosexuals than among heterosexuals.[36] That is the view most psychiatrists have recently come to hold. In 1973 the members of the American Psychiatric Association voted to stop classifying homosexuality as a mental or emotional disorder—even though, the members agree, *in some cases* that's just what it is. But in many other cases it is only a "sexual orientation disturbance"—a bent or deflected choice of partner, not a psychological illness.

Gay liberationists and some social scientists claim that the new studies prove that homosexuality is perfectly natural and healthy, and that the sickness theory is dead wrong. That's not what the studies show. They show that many gays had a somewhat troubled or disturbed family life as children, or had unhealthy relationships with one parent or the other. They strongly suggest that some of these gays developed emotional ailments as a result and that their homosexuality is a symptom of these ailments.[37] Even gays themselves sometimes say so: 27 percent of the male gays in one recent survey said they considered homosexuality an emotional disorder.[38]

But in the case of other homosexuals, childhood experiences, plus other causes, shaped them into homosexuals *without* making them emotionally ill. It's somewhat like the way some children grow up hating school because of bad experiences with poor or unpleasant teachers. Their feeling about school isn't a sickness, but it's certainly an "orientation disturbance"—they're oriented away from school, when most children are oriented toward it.

Thus, we cannot call emotional sickness *the* cause of homosexuality. It's *one* cause of *some kinds* of homosexuality, especially the strange, self-damaging, unloving kinds. But the same childhood experiences or parent-child troubles that make some children into sick homosexuals make others into apparently healthy homosexuals.

In any case, most authorities, whether they consider homosexuality an illness or not, or take the middle ground, agree that these special childhood experiences or parent-child troubles are the most important cause of homosexuality in our society today.

Natural impulse

Freud himself believed that every infant is capable of learning to respond sexually to persons of either sex; but in a normal family, he felt, the child is taught to ignore the homosexual side of his or her nature and to develop the heterosexual side. In recent years, many gays and some psychologists have extended this notion. The homosexual impulse, they say, is as natural a part of us as the heterosexual impulse, and we'd all have homosexual relationships if our society taught us that it was all right to do so. As proof that it's natural and normal, they point out that, among animals, males of many species often mount other males; in fact, this is most common among our closest relatives, the monkeys and the apes. As for human beings, in many other countries homosexuality is considered acceptable—and in any country where it is, many or most of the people engage in homosexual acts. One famous survey shows that in nearly two thirds of all primitive societies, homosexuality is permissible, at least for certain people or at certain times.[39] It has also been allowed in many civilized societies, and practiced by many people; this was true in ancient Greece and Rome, and in more recent centuries in China, Turkey, parts of India, and many Middle Eastern countries.

So it seems that, at birth, we are all capable of becoming bisexual or homosexual, rather than heterosexual, and that social approval or disapproval plays a big part in deciding whether we do or don't. If a child grows up in a society which says that it's all right to perform homosexual acts, he or she probably will feel and think that it is all right. If a child grows up in a society which says that homosexuality is dirty, perverted, and unnatural, he or she probably will feel and think so, too. (There always are exceptions—people who grow up to disagree with what their society says—but we're talking about how most people grow up.)

Thus, in many societies custom and tradition encourage the natural impulse to homosexual behavior. But in our own country, custom and tradition stifle the natural impulse and cause most people to avoid homosexual behavior. From this, it is obvious that the natural-impulse theory isn't enough to explain the homosexuality that exists in our society. There must be other reasons why some people follow that impulse despite strong social disapproval—and we have already seen what a number of those reasons are. We have seen that various combinations of at least six different causes seem to explain all, or nearly all, of the wide range of different homosexualities in our country.

One more thing, before we're done with the natural-impulse theory. Does the behavior of animals prove that homosexuality is as natural for them as heterosexuality? Does the fact that homosexuality is common in other societies mean that it is as natural for human beings as heterosexuality?

In one sense, yes—the sense that the potential for it is built into animals and people, and does not require emotional sickness to call it forth.

In another sense, no—the sense that under the usual conditions of life, most animals and most people tend to behave heterosexually rather than homosexually. And that's not because they're forced to, for even when they're free to do what they want, most of them *by nature* prefer heterosexual sex.

Many animals, to be sure, sometimes perform homosexual acts—but homosexuality is never their preferred form of sex. Most of the time it's only a form of play, or a way in which the tougher male shows that he's the boss and the weaker male makes peace with him. But it's almost never a complete sex act—the one who mounts rarely does more than give a few thrusts, without actually entering or having an orgasm, and then dismounts.[40]

For another thing, even in those societies which have been most easygoing about homosexuality, it has never been the main choice for men or women. It has never been as common as heterosexuality, and only rarely has it been thought to be as desirable as heterosexual lovemaking. In many of the societies that have allowed it, it has been considered all right only for young boys. In other societies, although it's been permitted for grown people, they have generally been considered a little odd in the head. They have been treated kindly but condescendingly. Even the berdaches and their husbands were thought amusing by most of those who tolerated them.[41]

So while there are homosexual possibilities in the natures of animals and human beings, the heterosexual possibilities in their natures are stronger and more likely to develop. Homosexuality is natural, but it isn't *as natural* as heterosexuality—that is, it isn't as likely to be the outcome of the ordinary experiences of growing up.

A fig tree, under ordinary conditions, grows up round. On a windy slope, it may take other shapes, and in a garden, the gardener may espalier it—train it flat against a sunny wall. The wind-swept tree and the espaliered tree aren't "unnatural," as a genetically deformed tree is; they have just developed in ways that are different from the usual way because of special influences at work. But in one sense the round tree is the more natural one: it has the shape most likely to develop in most conditions in which the tree lives and grows.

That's one way to think of the difference between homosexuality and heterosexuality.

Taste

One final explanation: some gays and even a few straights now claim that the real cause of homosexuality is merely a personal taste for it—that homosexuals simply like it better than heterosexuality. Here are two such statements, one by a gay liberation leader, the other by a young psychiatrist:

—Homosexuality is a preference not different in kind from heterosexuality, and fully on a par with it.

—Lesbianism is a way of life, not a sickness. The only difference between the lesbian and other women is the choice of love object.

But to say that people are homosexual because they prefer homosexuality to heterosexuality is to explain nothing. *Why* do they prefer it? There is a reason for every preference—and that reason is the cause of the behavior. If you like chocolate and dislike vanilla, it could be because your mother made you drink too many vanilla milk shakes when you were underweight. All over the world, the people of each country prefer certain kinds of foods and dislike the foods of other peoples— not because they have chosen freely among all possibilities, but because they were taught, as little children, to prefer the native foods of their own country.

So when we say we prefer one thing to another, it's not personal taste that is the real cause of what we do; that's only the last link in a chain of causes. As Professor John Money of Johns Hopkins University says, homosexuality isn't a condition that a person chooses; it's the long-term result of all the experiences he or she has in early childhood, acting upon his or her built-in tendencies.

Most people prefer simple explanations of things; this is why human beings have so often believed untruths, for the untrue explanation is frequently simpler than the true one. But what we have seen in this chapter shows us that the truth about what causes homosexuality is far from simple. Briefly, it can be summed up like this:

—There is no one cause of all homosexuality. There are a number of causes.

—Some causes tend to produce certain kinds of homosexuality, and other causes tend to produce other kinds.

—Often—perhaps most of the time—homosexuality is the result of several causes working together.

—In America today, the most significant cause of homosexuality—the one for which the evidence is strongest, the one which most often plays the largest part—is a faulty or distorted relationship between the growing child and one or both parents. Even so, such a relationship is usually not enough by itself to cause homosexuality; generally, the child has to be predisposed in some way. Yet the predisposing factors—physical, hormonal, and nervous conditions, for instance—rarely cause homosexuality by themselves: the essential thing is the child's life experience, especially within the family.

3

THE RIGHT

TO BE

GAY

What rights should gays have?
What rights do they have?

Do gays have a right to be gay?

The question isn't as simple as it sounds, because it's really two questions in one. First, should people have the right to perform sex acts with willing partners of their own sex? And second, if they do have that right, and do perform such sex acts, should they still have the same rights as other people to work at all sorts of jobs, to live where they like, to hold government positions, and to socialize publicly with other homosexuals?

If these questions didn't deal with an unusual sexual preference but with an unusual religious preference, most Americans would immediately answer yes to both of them. Yes, they'd say, everyone has a right to his own religious preference. Yes, they'd say, even if a person has an unusual religious preference, he should have all the other rights every American is entitled to.

But with sexual preference it's quite different. Even though most homosexual sex acts take place in private between freely consenting partners, most Americans feel that people have no right to perform them. And most Americans feel that people who do perform them don't deserve the same civil and social rights as other citizens.

Here, for instance, are half a dozen statements about homosexual rights which were part of a recent national survey.[42] See how many you agree with or disagree with; then you'll be able to tell where you stand as compared with the majority of adult Americans.

—There should be a law against sex acts between persons of the same sex.

—Sex between two persons of the same sex is wrong if they have no special affection for each other.

—Sex between two persons of the same sex is wrong even if they love each other.

—Homosexuals should not be allowed to teach school.

—Homosexuals should not be allowed to hold positions in the government.

—Homosexuals should not be allowed to dance with each other in public places.

If you more or less agree with all six statements, you have the average American attitude toward gay rights; a large majority of Americans in the survey approved of each of these statements. If you agree *very strongly* with some or all of them, you're more conservative than the average American. But if you disagree with some or all of them, you're more liberal than the average American.

It wouldn't be surprising if you found that you were more liberal than the average American in this survey. For one thing, the survey was conducted in 1970, and most of us have grown a bit more liberal since then in our attitudes toward sex before marriage, the kinds of sexual acts suitable for lovers and married people, and homosexuality. These changes are part of the movements known as women's liberation, the sexual revolution, and gay liberation.

For another thing, there's a good reason why you might be more liberal about gay rights than the average person—namely, your age. In every major sex survey of recent years, young people have shown themselves to be more liberal than the middle-aged or the elderly. In part that's because most people become more conservative about sex as they grow older. In part it's because the middle-aged and the elderly cling to many of the attitudes that were common when they were growing up, while young people tend to adopt the newer attitudes that are becoming popular in their own time.

But the newer attitudes are still too new, and held by too few people, to have brought about equality of civil rights for gays. In the late 1970's in most parts of America, gays are still second-class citizens who lack many of the civil rights that have recently been won by blacks and other minority groups, and by women. For instance:

—In a large majority of states, most of the sexual techniques used by homosexual men and by lesbians are classified as felonies (serious crimes).[43] In over a dozen states, the penalty for mouth-genital contact or for anal intercourse can be as much as ten to fifteen years in prison; in another dozen states, the penalty can be more than fifteen years; and in a few it can even be life imprisonment. The "sodomy statutes" (laws against sodomy) are supposedly aimed at heterosexuals as well as homosexuals; these sex acts are illegal no matter who performs them with whom. But even though many husbands and wives (and many unmarried lovers) nowadays include some of these sex acts in their lovemaking, the laws are enforced only against homosexuals, never against heterosexuals (unless rape is involved).

—In most states, homosexuals who publicly hold hands, kiss, or dance together can be arrested and fined or given minor jail sentences for "disorderly conduct" or for "lewd and lascivious behavior."[44] Laws of this sort are enforced against homosexuals much more often than the sodomy statutes. Heterosexuals, of course, run no such risk. Homosexuals are also often arrested on disorderly-conduct charges for inviting plain-clothes policemen (posing as possible pickups) to have sex with them, but heterosexuals—except for prostitutes—are almost never arrested for similar behavior.

—A male or female gay has no right to enlist in or remain in the armed forces. If a person in any of the armed forces admits to being homosexual, or is proven to be so, he or she is automatically given a "general" (less than honorable) discharge. Each year, many hundreds of persons are disgraced and damaged by being thrown out of military service under these regulations.[45]

—Many employers will not hire a person they believe or know to be homosexual, even if that person is fully qualified for the job. Many employers will fire a person they believe or know to be homosexual, even if the person has been doing his or her work properly in every way. Federal laws protect women, blacks, and middle-aged people from unfairness in hiring and firing, but there is no federal or state law to protect the rights of gays.[46] About one out of every six male gays has had employment problems, and one out of ten has lost a job, because of his homosexuality.[47]

—Many landlords will not rent to people they think are gay, and in many restaurants people who appear to be gay get poor service or are refused service altogether. Federal laws, and the laws of some states and cities, prevent landlords and restaurant owners from discriminating against people on the basis of race or sex, but as of the late 1970's there were no similar federal or state laws to protect gays, and only a few cities had passed laws prohibiting such discrimination.[48]

These are only a few of the ways in which our society denies homosexuals important civil rights that straights possess. But beyond these civil rights, gays lack many of the social rights the rest of us take for granted, such as the right to be treated with ordinary good manners and respect, the right to be a part of everyday socializing, and the right to be looked upon as equals of other people. In most parts of American society, homosexuals are treated in ways ranging from half-hidden scorn to open hatred. People avoid them, exclude them, whisper or joke about them, stare at them with open hostility. Vandals sometimes write nasty words on their cars, or wreck their homes or business places, and bullies sometimes beat them up and seriously injure them. The families of some homosexuals refuse to have anything to do with them; the families of many others pretend not to know, and the homosexual goes along with the pretense —but feels their silent contempt.

One of the most important social rights the gay lacks is the right to be judged according to his or her deeds, rather than according to some preconceived idea of what kind of person he or she must be. The black who is assumed to be stupid and lazy, the Jew who is assumed to be money-grubbing and dishonest, are humiliated at being prejudged and not dealt with as the persons they really are. The same thing is true of homosexuals: no matter how upright a homosexual may be in his dealings with other people, his straight friends may sometimes unintentionally reveal that they secretly suspect him of having a bad character, of lacking any moral decency. Merle Miller, in his book *On Being Different*, gives a painful example of this. He was expecting a heterosexual friend—a man who had known him for twenty-five years —to come out for the weekend with his sixteen-year-old son. On the afternoon when the friend was to arrive, he phoned Miller to say he wouldn't be bringing his son after all. Miller asked why. The friend mumbled something to the effect that his son was "only an impressionable kid"; then he tried to fix up the slip by adding, "While I've known you and know you wouldn't, but suppose you had some friends in, and . . ." Miller, humiliated and hurt, told his friend to stay home, too.

For all these reasons, the great majority of homosexuals remain "in the closet" (keep their homosexuality a secret from everyone who is not gay). Various observers estimate that anywhere from two thirds to nine tenths of all male and female homosexuals are still in the closet even now, despite years of effort by the gay liberation movement to get them to come out.[49]

Remaining in the closet, for fear of being penalized by society, is said by some gays to be the worst part of being gay.

It means living a lie all day long and constantly being afraid of accidentally saying something or making some gesture that will give one away, that will let the "terrible truth" slip out.

It means living in continual fear of some chance meeting, in a public place, with an obviously gay acquaintance, or of exposure through blackmail. (One out of every ten gay men has been blackmailed.[50])

It means going out to public places with a friend, lover, or life companion, and being unable to sit close to each other, look fondly at each other, or hold hands, for fear of being stared at in contempt or anger—or even of being arrested.

It means laughing at the anti-gay jokes that straight people make, in order to seem to be one of them—and hating them for their attitude, and oneself for one's cowardice.

It means hiding many of your deepest emotions from straight people—and knowing that, as a result, they pityingly think you have no feelings at all. One lesbian says that she can't reveal to her fellow workers either that she's in love and happy or that she's out of love and wretched. "They must think I never feel anything deeply," she says. "No doubt they think I am so cold no one could ever love me, or I them."

No wonder three quarters of the gays in one recent survey said they often or nearly always have trouble falling asleep, half said they sometimes or often drink too much, two thirds said that often their hands tremble enough to bother them, and four out of ten said that at times they feel they are going to have a nervous breakdown.[51]

One gay liberationist said a while ago that he didn't care whether straights liked him or not as long as he got the rights he was entitled to. But another gay said, sadly, that that wasn't good enough for him; he wanted to be liked, too. For although you won't find the right to be liked in the Constitution or in the laws of any state, it is as important as any right that exists—and as any right that gays lack.

The persecution of gays: An ancient tradition

Our American intolerance of homosexuality is unusual; most peoples throughout the world have been more tolerant of it than we are. But it is an old tradition in our society; it goes back thousands of years to the ancient Hebrews, whose attitudes and way of life are set down in the earliest books of the Old Testament.

For it is in Genesis 13:13 that we read of the men of the city of Sodom, who were "wicked and sinners before

the Lord exceedingly" because they practiced homosexuality. (This is how the sodomy statutes got their
name and why male homosexuals were once commonly
called sodomites.) All the men of Sodom gathered one
night to force their sexual attentions on two guests in
the house of Lot—angels who appeared to be men. The
angels protected Lot and themselves by striking the
Sodomites with blindness, and the next day the Lord
rained brimstone and fire down on Sodom and another
wicked city, Gomorrah, and totally destroyed them.

That sums up the ancient Judeo-Christian attitude
toward homosexuality. Leviticus 20:13 makes homosexual acts illegal and sets a harsh penalty: "If a man also
lie with mankind, as he lieth with a woman, both of
them have committed an abomination: they shall surely
be put to death; their blood shall be upon them." (The
Old Testament says nothing directly about lesbianism,
probably because it seemed unimportant to the ancient
Jews. But theirs was a strongly patriarchal society, and
male homosexuality challenged their notions of masculinity and seemed an attack on God Himself, since man
was made in His image. Indeed, throughout Western
history, female homosexuality has been less harshly condemned than male homosexuality.)

In the early days of Christianity, the Church Fathers
took a less extreme stand. They did not assert that
homosexuals should be put to death; that had been
Hebrew law, and the Christians were living under
Roman law, which was far more tolerant of sexual variations. But they did preach and write that homosexuality
was a grave sin, and that homosexuals could not enter
heaven and would surely be punished by hellfire. St.

Augustine, and later St. Thomas Aquinas, two of the greatest interpreters of Catholicism, explained why homosexuality was such a terrible sin: God's purpose in giving men and women sexual organs was to ensure the creation of children; for a man to have sex with a man (or a woman with a woman) was to transgress against Divine law and to commit a crime against nature—the nature that God had created.

Several of the Christian emperors of Rome passed laws against homosexuality, but it remained for the Emperor Justinian, in the year 538, to set the legal standard for the next thirteen centuries in Europe. Justinian, a devout Christian, decreed that homosexuals were to be tortured, castrated, paraded in public, and then burned at the stake. Later on, the Church, too, resorted to violence against homosexuals: in the Middle Ages, Church inquisitors tortured homosexuals until they confessed to heresy—to taking part in homosexual ceremonies that profaned the cross and mocked the Christian Mass. And having confessed, they were burned alive.

After the Middle Ages, homosexuality gradually ceased to be regarded as a heresy, but it remained a serious crime, and as late as the eighteenth century homosexuals were still occasionally tried as criminals and burned at the stake. In the nineteenth century, when Napoleon revised the laws of France, homosexual acts performed in private ceased to be a crime in that country. But in many other European countries—including Germany, Austria, Russia, and England—and in the United States, homosexual acts remained felonies and still are today in most of those countries and in most of the states of the United States.[52]

These harsh laws, and the public attitudes that went with them, never stamped out homosexuality at any time, but they did make most homosexuals live in constant fear and keep their homosexuality secret. Throughout the centuries, they lived a double life—having one set of desires and feelings but pretending to have another, and knowing that, in the eyes of the world, the real person hidden inside was vile, criminal, and contemptible.

Most homosexuals accepted this public view of homosexuality—what other view was there?—and despised themselves. Even as recently as a century ago, the self-hatred of homosexuals was so strong that many of them felt suicidal, according to Dr. Richard von Krafft-Ebing, a nineteenth-century expert in sexual matters. One suffering man wrote to him as follows:

> You have no idea what a constant struggle we all must endure, and how we suffer. The youthful homosexual sees men that attract him, but he dares not say—nay, not even betray by a look—what his feelings are. He thinks that he alone of all the world has such abnormal feelings. Or let us suppose that the homosexual has had the rare fortune to find a person like himself. But he cannot be approached openly, as a lover approaches the girl he loves. In constant fear, both must conceal their relations. Even in this relation is forged a chain of anxiety and fear that the secret will be betrayed or discovered, which leaves them no joy in the indulgence. Anyone with an adequate idea of the mental and moral suffering, of the anxiety and care that the homosexual must endure, can only be surprised that more insanity and nervous disturbance do not occur.

That was in Germany, where the law was extremely severe. But in England, where it was less severe, a homosexual could still feel much the same way—in particular, could feel horror and disgust with himself for being a person all society despised. Only about eighty years ago, one man wrote to the sex researcher Havelock Ellis, explaining that while his homosexual drive was tremendously strong, he fought it desperately because he was so revolted at the thought of the things he desired to do:

> I have not hitherto betrayed my abnormal instinct. I have never made any person the victim of passion: moral and religious feelings were too powerful. My friendships with men, younger men, have been colored by passion, against which I have fought continually. The shame of this has made life a hell, and the horror of this abnormality has been an enemy to my religious faith. I cannot discover that friendship with younger men can go uncolored by a sensuous admixture which fills me with shame and loathing.

Liberalism: The new tradition

The ancient anti-homosexual tradition finally started to break down a little over a century ago. As we saw in the previous chapter, a few doctors began to think that homosexuality was a hereditary disease rather than a sin or a crime. In 1887, Dr. Krafft-Ebing concluded his study of the subject by calling for the repeal of the German law punishing homosexuality; one should not punish a sickness, he said. Later, Sigmund Freud, Havelock Ellis, and others also considered homosexuality a psychological defect; they didn't agree as to the cause—and some of them didn't believe it could be cured—but all of them felt that it was neither a crime nor a sin, and that homosexuals should be treated with tolerance and compassion. At the same time, various writers and social scientists began to describe the acceptance of homosexuality in many societies outside Europe and America. A relatively tolerant attitude toward homosexuality began to catch on with the well-educated part of the public in various countries. Among other results, the penalties for homosexuality were somewhat eased in certain European countries and in some states of our own country, and even where harsh laws remained in effect they were rarely enforced.[53]

By the 1940's most well-educated people in America had come to think of homosexuality as a disease or abnormality. Many of them thought themselves tolerant of homosexuals, although the idea of homosexual acts still disgusted them and few of them would have homosexuals as friends. As for the less-educated majority of Americans, most of them still considered homosexuality sinful or criminal, or both.

But in 1949 and 1953, Dr. Alfred C. Kinsey and his co-workers published the first results of their huge survey of American sexual behavior—and shocked the American public by revealing that something like a third of all American men and a fifth of all American women had had some homosexual experiences at some time in their lives.[54] (Most of this, to be sure, was only childish or adolescent "fooling around" that did not continue into adult life.) The average American was also astounded to learn that one out of every three single men over the age of thirty and one out of every fourteen single women over thirty were largely or completely homosexual. If so many people had had homosexual experiences before adulthood, and if so many people were homosexuals in adulthood, homosexuality couldn't be as uniformly vile, as totally abnormal, as people had thought. The Kinsey findings, repeated in countless articles and books, didn't turn the average American into a liberal on this matter, but they did make him begin to wonder about and doubt some of his beliefs. They built a foundation for a new attitude that would finally begin to take hold in the 1970's.

Meanwhile, some doctors and social scientists were taking a giant step beyond the early liberalism. At first, it had seemed liberal to classify homosexuality as an emotional disorder rather than as a sin or a crime, but by the 1960's a few sex researchers began to argue that even this was a subtle way of condemning homosexual behavior. Only about one quarter of homosexual patients gave up their homosexuality as a result of treatment;[55] perhaps the rest weren't sick at all. Maybe it wasn't a disease; maybe, as anthropologists who had seen it in other societies said, much of it was a *variation* rather than a sickness. Dr. Kinsey himself had strenuously fought the view that homosexuality is an "abnormal and unnatural" kind of human sexual behavior.

Most psychologists and social scientists thought Kinsey was too extreme in his views. Certainly, in our own society many homosexuals seemed to have definite emotional ailments. But, said the more liberal scientists, maybe these ailments weren't necessarily part of the homosexuality itself; maybe some or even most of the ailments were due to the anxiety and fear homosexuals felt about being exposed and hounded by society. By the 1960's a handful of doctors and social scientists had begun to think that the best way to deal with the emotional problems of most homosexuals wasn't to try to change them into heterosexuals but to change the society around them. The best way to cure most of the emotional ailments of homosexuals would be to make heterosexual people truly tolerant, so that homosexuals could be free of the need for secrecy, could live comfortable and liberated lives, could belong to the world around them. But this view still seemed far too radical to the great majority of straight people, including most of the well-educated and the liberal.

Gay liberation

Thus, as late as the 1960's, homosexuals were still a persecuted and oppressed minority. Things were less dreadful for them than in the nineteenth century, but they still lacked many basic civil rights. If they were out of the closet, they were very often treated with contempt or hostility; if they were in the closet, they lived in constant fear of exposure. Like the majority of Americans, many of them considered homosexuality a defect, abnormality, or disease, and many disliked or even detested themselves. In a few areas of American life—show business, the art world, the fashion world—homosexuals were relatively well accepted and could be somewhat more open. But elsewhere, in most social circles and nearly all American communities, life was as intolerable for an open or known homosexual as it would have been for a black in a wealthy, "lily-white" neighborhood in the South or in a racist, working-class neighborhood in, say, Boston.

In 1965, 82 percent of the men and 58 percent of the women in a national poll said that homosexuals were harmful to the nation; only Communists and atheists were rated worse.[56] In that same poll, the great majority of people felt that homosexual acts, even in private between consenting partners, should remain illegal. Even in 1970, a majority of Americans in the national sample mentioned at the beginning of this chapter felt that homosexuals should not be permitted to work as teachers, ministers, judges, doctors, or government employees.[57] Two thirds of the people in the same survey said they had never liked homosexuals, and four out of five said they did not want to associate with them.

The vast majority of homosexuals still lived with the constant tension of keeping their homosexuality secret from the entire straight world, as if they were spies in an enemy land. As one lesbian wrote in 1970:[58]

The worst part of being a homosexual is having to keep it *secret*. Not the occasional murders by police or teenage queer-beaters, not the loss of jobs or expulsion from schools or dishonorable discharges—but the daily knowledge that what you are is so awful that it cannot be revealed . . . This is what tears us apart, what makes us want to stand up in the offices, in the factories and schools and shout out our true identities.

No wonder Dr. Bieber and several other psychiatrists said, in the 1960's, that they did not believe there were any truly happy homosexuals.

No wonder a character in the 1968 play *The Boys in the Band* says, "You show me a happy homosexual, and I'll show you a gay corpse." (Most of the male gays interviewed by sociologist Martin Weinberg of the Institute for Sexual Research in the late 1960's said they definitely agreed with that statement.)

No wonder four out of five male gays who were members of a homosexual organization said, a few years ago, that if they had a son, they wouldn't want him to be a homosexual.[59]

No wonder one homosexual doctor, who used to hide his homosexuality from everyone (including his wife, his father, and the firm which employed him as company doctor), says of that period of his life, "I used to wish I could wake up dead some mornings."

And then came gay liberation.[60]

In a way, it had been coming for many years. The liberal influences we have just discussed had been clearing the way. In a few states, the laws against homosexuals were eased or erased during the 1960's. In the 1950's and 1960's, liberal church groups in several cities set up committees to help homosexuals with their emotional and everyday problems. A few homosexuals began, timidly at first, to create self-help organizations of their own. The Mattachine Society (male gays) and the

Daughters of Bilitis (lesbians) were both organized in the 1950's primarily to help gays who were in trouble, and by the 1960's had begun to fight for the civil rights of all gays and to try to change the attitude of the public. Other gay organizations sprang up in many cities and on various college campuses until, by 1970, there were at least a hundred of them around the country.

They drew some of their courage from the newer medical and sociological view of homosexuality. But they drew even more of it from the example of other groups that had been fighting for the civil rights of minorities, especially the black civil rights movement and the women's liberation movement. It made sense to the more daring gays to fight openly for their own civil rights, and to try to take their message to the general public. That meant coming out in the open—but there was no other way to start a mass civil-rights movement.

At first, they limited themselves to a few demonstrations and picket lines, and a few lawsuits against employers who were unfair to gays in their hiring and firing practices. But pressure was building up, and on a hot summer night the lid blew off. On June 28, 1969, the police raided the Stonewall, a gay bar in New York City's Greenwich Village. It started out much like any other police raid on a gay bar—but this time, without any advance planning, the gays began to fight back. They threw cans and rocks at the police, locked them in the bar and set it on fire, and then fought with other police in the streets for hours. The "Stonewall Rebellion" touched off a militant stage in the gay liberation movement. A group of daring young gays founded the Gay Liberation

Front and organized huge marches and demonstrations. On the first anniversary of the Stonewall Rebellion, thousands of gay men and women marched in the streets of New York, Chicago, and Los Angeles, chanting "Shout it loud, gay is proud," and "Three, five, seven, nine, lesbians are mighty fine." They invited onlookers to join them, they hugged each other, they mugged at the news cameras, they dared anyone to make trouble—but no one did. Nothing like it had ever been seen before in the history of America, or even of Christian civilization. (The anniversary parades have been held every year since, and have spread to San Francisco, Boston, and several other cities.)

During the next few years, a number of well-known people came out of the closet, among them Kate Millett, a leading feminist; the novelist Gore Vidal; the playwright Tennessee Williams; Dave Kopay, a long-time pro-football player; and the late Dr. Howard Brown, a high official in the New York City government. Gay activist organizations multiplied and grew; by 1975 there were eight hundred of them. On many campuses, gays fought for—and won—the right to have meeting places of their own and to give gay dances. Lesbians struggled to seize control of the women's movement, were all but thrown out of its biggest organization, N.O.W., and then were made welcome within it.

By now, the members of the gay pressure groups have copied most of the techniques of other civil rights organizations. They have marched, picketed, and carried signs; have sent delegates and lobbyists to Washington, written thousands of letters to lawmakers, and started lawsuits against employers; have published articles and books, appeared on television talk shows, and held press conferences. A handful of gays in the military, including one fairly high-ranking officer (Commander Gary Hess of the U.S. Naval Reserve), have openly identified themselves as homosexuals and fought their discharges from the service in the courts—unsuccessfully, so far.

All this hasn't yet won as much for gays as it has for blacks and women. But that's understandable: gay liberation is still very new, the traditional dislike of gays is tremendously strong, and the great majority of gays are still afraid to come out and take part in the movement.

But all the same, things *have* changed dramatically since the mid-1960's. Here are a few of the changes:

—Homosexuals never used to be shown in movies except as sick people or villains, or persons who came to a bad end; inevitably, they were exposed and often they committed suicide. But in the 1960's and even more so in the 1970's they began to be portrayed in more varied and realistic ways—the good-hearted hustler in *Midnight Cowboy*, the kind, loving physician in *Sunday Bloody Sunday*, and so on.

—Plays and books about homosexuality have been published more freely than ever. Some are trashy, some serious and worthwhile. Most interesting, however, is the fact that in novels homosexuals are more frequently portrayed as whole human beings—perhaps troubled by their sexual preference, perhaps not, but in any case sympathetic characters. One novel has as its hero a homosexual detective, another a non-violent and quite charming "cat burglar," another a college track-team coach.

—The long-standing taboo against the discussion or portrayal of homosexuality on television ended in the 1970's. First, homosexuality was openly discussed—with gay liberationists, among others—on late-night talk shows. Next, it was dealt with candidly and fairly on documentaries earlier in the evening. Finally, by 1976, homosexuals were appearing as characters—often sympathetic —in situation comedies in prime viewing time.

—Although the Catholic Church still condemns all homosexual acts, in 1976 it gave official permission to a Jesuit priest, Father John McNeill, to publish a book— *The Church and the Homosexual*—in which he disagrees with the Church's position. Father McNeill maintains that if love is involved, homosexuality is as moral as heterosexuality.

—The American Psychiatric Association (as we saw earlier) voted in 1973 to cease classifying homosexuality as a psychiatric disorder and to reclassify it as a "sexual orientation disturbance." (In other words, some or even many—but not all—homosexuals are psychologically healthy.) Many gays are feeling somewhat better about themselves as a result; more important, the general public is very likely to accept the new medical view over a period of time.

—In a number of cities—nearly thirty by 1976—including Washington, D.C., Detroit, Minneapolis, and San Francisco, "homosexual rights laws" of one sort or another have been passed.[61] The stronger ones assure gays of equal rights to jobs, equal rights to housing, and equal rights to public accommodations such as restaurants. Of course, under thirty cities is only a small beginning—but it *is* a beginning. Far more important, in July 1975 the U.S. Civil Service Commission formally dropped its historic policy of not hiring homosexuals for government jobs.

—Since 1962, one quarter of the states in our country have repealed their sodomy statutes, making it legal for consenting adults—whether straight or gay—to perform in private those acts that have so long been called crimes against nature.[62] Many lawyers expected the Supreme Court to rule, sooner or later, that state laws against sodomy are unconstitutional because they invade the individual's right to privacy. This would have wiped out all such laws remaining in the rest of the states. Instead, in March 1976, the Supreme Court ruled that the states do have the right to pass such laws and enforce them. This did not put the laws back into effect where they had been repealed, but it somewhat slowed down the drive toward repeal in other states. Nevertheless, it still seems likely that the sodomy statutes will continue to be repealed, state by state, over the coming years.

—In 1975 the Department of Defense granted a homosexual employee, Otis Tabler, clearance to be entrusted with secret materials. Previously, the department held that homosexuals shouldn't have such clearance because they could be blackmailed into revealing secrets to enemy governments. But Tabler openly announced that he was gay, and said in court that, because he had nothing to hide, he couldn't be blackmailed. The court agreed. A number of other gays employed in the Department of Defense have followed his lead and applied for similar clearance.

—In 1974, Elaine Noble of Boston, an out-of-the-closet

lesbian, won election to the Massachusetts legislature.

The gay liberation movement is still far from having achieved its goal of full civil and social rights throughout the nation. But it has begun to change the feelings that gays have long had about themselves, and those that the straight world has long had about them. We are at the end of an era in our history and at the beginning of a new one—an era in which our society, like many other societies, will come to tolerate homosexuals, will cease to discriminate against them, and will use police power and criminal penalties only against those who are criminal or dangerous. Eventually, homosexuals will almost certainly win the same civil and social rights now enjoyed by heterosexuals—including the right to have the kind of sex they prefer, with the persons they choose.

The effects of gay liberation

It's much too soon for gay liberation to have made major changes in the lives of most gays, or to have transformed their relationships with the straights around them. The great majority of gays, as we have seen, are still in the closet. But many more than formerly are now out of the closet, living openly and unashamedly as their real selves. Many of the gays who have been growing up in these past few years have far less guilt about their homosexuality than older gays—or no guilt at all. As Merle Miller puts it, "For thousands of young homosexuals, and some not so young, the quiet desperation that [psychiatrist Martin] Hoffman talks about is all over. They are neither quiet nor desperate." Here's some evidence:

—Even though most male gays in a recent survey said they often had trouble falling asleep, and were bothered by trembling hands, two thirds of them said nevertheless that, on the whole, they considered themselves quite happy.[63]

—Over half the gays in this survey denied wishing that they weren't homosexuals. Three quarters of them disagreed with the idea that homosexuality is a mental illness. The gays who regard homosexuality as psychologically normal are less bothered by outside opinions of it and therefore have fewer emotional problems than those who do consider it an illness.

—In scores of articles and books, and in any number of appearances on radio and TV, out-of-the-closet gays have told of the immense relief they felt when they no longer had to pretend, to conceal the truth, and to despise themselves for it.

—Even closet gays are probably helped to some extent by the newer attitudes they see gaining ground. Though they haven't come out, they have less reason than formerly to think ill of themselves for being homosexual.

And what effect is all this likely to have on straight society?

First, we've already seen that gay liberation hasn't yet increased the total number of homosexuals. Whether it will do so in the future no one knows, but most liberal sex researchers believe that it will not. In fact, Dr. John Money of Johns Hopkins University believes that the easing of taboos on sex in general—especially premarital sex between males and females—will cause heterosexuality to gain, and homosexuality to *decrease*, in the future.[64]

Second, many heterosexuals are coming to feel more at ease about homosexuality and homosexuals as a result of the new openness. Where there is no concealment, there is no sense of tension. Friendship between straights and gays becomes possible when neither is being false, when neither is hiding the truth, when each respects the right of the other to be what he or she is. The more they mingle socially, the easier it gets; straight males used to fear that if they were seen with gay males, they would be taken to be gay, but this is beginning to die away. And as straights find themselves mixing easily with gays—at least, with those who don't look or act especially "queer"—they begin to see them as total human beings and not only as sexually different human beings.

Lastly, will gay liberation do any damage to our society? The majority of Americans still fear it may. Many of them think that the growing acceptance of homosexuality is a major factor in the growing avoidance of marriage and family life. Some authorities, such as psychiatrist Herbert Hendin, a professor at Columbia University, flatly call homosexuality "socially disruptive." But most authorities strongly disagree. If gay liberation hasn't increased the number of homosexuals, it can't be the cause of the decline of family life. The real threat to marriage and family life is the tendency of straights to avoid marriage and parenthood so as to remain "free," but even this threat has been much exaggerated. In any case, we know from examples all around the world that homosexuality can and does coexist with heterosexuality and marriage, and that it has never caused any society to stop producing and raising children. As Dr. Judd Marmor, president of the American Psychiatric Association, pointed out in reply to Dr. Hendin, "In countries such as the Netherlands, West Germany and Denmark, where homosexuality is acceptable, there are no indications that family stability has been impaired."[65]

The most serious threat to our society arising from gay liberation is that we may believe the exaggerated and unscientific claims of the radical gay liberationists. They would have us believe—and they may actually convince people who don't know better—that everyone is homosexual at heart and those who don't try it are cowardly or "hung up." Or that a man and woman can never love each other as completely and tenderly as a man and a man, or a woman and a woman. Or that homosexual sex is better and more enjoyable than heterosexual sex. Or that gays are not only as mentally healthy as straights but more so.

All of these claims have been made in print by a number of gays and by a few of their straight friends. But all are propaganda, not scientific fact. They are the prejudices of the gay militants against straights—and they are no better, and no truer, than the prejudices that straights have long had against gays.

But we can hope that as gays become more thoroughly liberated, they will no longer be angry at the straight world, and will no longer need to believe or to spout such propaganda. We can hope that some day straights and gays—like whites and blacks, and men and women—will become true equals, and will be able to live together in friendship and mutual respect.

4

BUT WHAT

DO THEY DO?

The mystery of homosexual sex

The one thing every straight person knows about homo-sexuality is that it involves sex acts between partners of the same sex. But while everyone knows this, many straight people are mystified by it. Young people in par-ticular are often unable to figure out how it works. They wonder what it is that homosexuals actually *do* sexually, and many of them suppose that it must consist of strange, unnatural, or even dreadful physical acts.

It's not surprising that they feel this way. They learn during childhood that the man's body and the woman's body are tailored to fit each other sexually, and that this is the result of millions of years of evolution. Most young people know, by the time they reach their teens, that during sexual excitement the man's penis becomes stiff and capable of being inserted into the woman's vagina, and that the vagina becomes moist and capable of comfortably receiving his penis. They know, too, that the movement of the penis in the vagina during intercourse excites each partner more and more until it results in the explosive moment of pleasure called orgasm, and that this is followed by peace and satisfaction.

But what can two men do together, or what can two women do together, that could be anything like this? How can two male bodies, or two female bodies, fit together in sex? What on earth do homosexuals do?

The whole subject is perplexing only because our society has kept it secret. For many centuries, the sex acts of homosexuals were considered so vile and disgusting that they were never talked about, described, or even mentioned aloud or in print. In fact, in many of the states that outlaw homosexual acts, the lawmakers could not bring themselves to name the particular acts they were making crimes. The laws in those states never say what the forbidden acts are but only allude to them in such vague terms as:

—unnatural carnal copulation;

—unnatural and lascivious acts;

—infamous crime against nature;

—abominable and detestable crime against nature.

No wonder homosexual sex acts are a mystery to most people.

But there's really very little that's strange or unusual about them except that they're performed by two persons of the same sex. Most of the same physical acts are also used by the majority of straight persons, usually as preliminaries to heterosexual intercourse but sometimes in place of it. The sodomy statutes that still exist in most states make it just as much a crime for heterosexuals, including husbands and wives, to use these sexual techniques as for homosexuals to do so.

That's because these acts can give great pleasure to straights as well as gays—and in our society, since the early days of Christianity, nearly all forms of sexual pleasure have been considered evil. Only vaginal intercourse between husbands and wives was considered acceptable, since it was necessary to create children. But all forms of sexual pleasure that did not or could not produce children were considered lustful and wicked. And so the Church called them sins, and lawmakers made them crimes.

As a result, for many centuries most people were afraid to do, or felt guilty about doing, many of the things that today are considered natural and desirable in lovemaking. For instance, until not so long ago—when your own parents were children—a good many husbands and wives could not bring themselves to touch or caress each other's sex organs. Many husbands rarely touched or kissed their wives' breasts. And a majority of husbands and wives never, in all their married lives, contacted each other's sex organs with their mouths.[66]

But in the past generation Americans have become far freer in the way they think about such things and in what they actually do. Many of the sex acts that most people used to shy away from and consider disgusting are now widely performed and considered beautiful. Today nearly all husbands and wives freely touch and caress each other's sex organs. Nearly all husbands now regularly touch and kiss their wives' breasts. And these days a large majority of husbands and wives have mouth-genital contact with each other at least now and then, and some do so regularly.[67] Of course, much the same thing is true of the sexual behavior of unmarried lovers.

Basically, those are the same acts that homosexuals perform: most of the sexual techniques used by homosexuals are not special to them but are also part of heterosexual lovemaking. (There is one exception: anal intercourse is used by many male gays but by few straight men and women. We'll come back to this later on.) Many straight people find it upsetting to read about or see pictures of homosexuals performing any of those acts, but it isn't the acts themselves so much as the persons performing them that they find bothersome. Heterosexuals may be as disgusted by a picture of two men kissing as by a picture of two men performing any of the typical homosexual sex acts.

What are those sex acts, and how widely is each used by homosexuals?

The techniques of homosexual lovemaking

A word of warning. Some readers may be upset by certain details in the following descriptions of sexual techniques commonly used by homosexuals. Nevertheless, there is no way to tell the truth about homosexuality without being specific about the sexual practices it involves.

These descriptions should not be taken as a how-to manual or as encouragement to experiment. No one should try out any sexual technique with any partner—

whether of the opposite sex or the same sex—without a full understanding of the emotional and social consequences such an act may have.

In each society, people have favorite sexual techniques, just as they have favorite foods, colors, and kinds of music. This is as true of homosexuals as of heterosexuals. What follows is a description of the sexual practices of male and female gays in the United States today; in other places and at other times, homosexual persons have avoided some of these practices, or preferred some that are not the favorites of homosexuals today.

Body contact: The simplest male homosexual sex practice consists of hugging, kissing, and rubbing the bodies together. It is chiefly the young and inexperienced who limit themselves to this technique, but for them it can be very pleasurable. It's much the same for them as it is for teen-age boys and girls who at first find general body contact extremely exciting even if they are dressed, and even more so if they are not. Like these boys and girls, young homosexuals vaguely imitate intercourse by pressing against each other in the genital area, and moving back and forth. But this is not a widely used or favorite technique for adult male gays;[68] for full satisfaction, including orgasm, the male generally needs to have the penis enclosed.

Lesbians, on the other hand, find body contact more satisfactory, since the mere pressure of their external parts against each other causes strong and pleasurable sensations in the clitoris and often is enough to produce orgasm. According to Dr. Kinsey, more than half of all lesbians use this technique when they are new to gay sex.[69] Even after years of experience, some continue to prefer it to more advanced techniques, but the majority of experienced lesbians use body contact only as a first step in lovemaking and after a short time go on to the other activities. (A more recent, but far smaller, survey shows that about a third of adult lesbians use body contact, but that nearly all of them also use other techniques.[70])

Mutual masturbation: A large majority of male gays rely on this technique early in their homosexual lives, and most adult male gays continue to use it as a preliminary to other activities.[71] Each partner masturbates the other by hand just as he would himself, either in turn or at the same time. Those who rely on this technique alone use it until it produces orgasm; others use it as a preliminary and move on to other methods as their excitement grows.

For lesbians, mutual masturbation is the most important sexual technique, not only early in their experience, but all their lives. It is generally accompanied by kissing, and by fondling of the breasts. Each partner masturbates the other by hand just as she would herself, or as a male masturbates a female. Many lesbians find that mutual masturbation to orgasm is deeply satisfying. Practically all lesbians use this technique at least part of the time, either simultaneously or by turns, and a small number of lesbians never use any other.[72]

Mouth-genital contact (*"oral sex"*): In many other lands, mouth-genital contact between men and women has been permissible, and in some places it has been considered a useful and desirable part of lovemaking. But in our own society, as we have seen, for many centuries most people regarded it as perverted and wicked. In the past thirty years this has changed greatly. The 1972 survey mentioned earlier showed that both of the mouth-genital techniques are now being used by well over half of American husbands and wives.[73]

These two techniques are known as *fellatio* and *cunnilingus*. Fellatio consists of kissing and mouthing a male partner's penis. Cunnilingus consists of kissing a female partner's sexual parts and stimulating them with the tongue. In most of today's sex and marriage manuals, both of these acts are viewed as normal variations of lovemaking. Each, it is said, can express deep intimacy and create intense sexual feeling in both partners.

Fellatio and cunnilingus are of particular importance to homosexuals. For males, fellatio offers a substitute for the vagina that neither partner has. For females, cunnilingus offers a substitute for the penis that neither partner has. In several recent surveys, the great majority of male homosexuals said that they use fellatio; most of them both "do" other males and are "done" by them.[74] Sometimes male homosexuals perform fellatio on each other at the same time; this is commonly called "69" because the positions of the partners are like those of the 6 and the 9.

Cunnilingus is as widely used by lesbians as fellatio is by male gays. Half of young lesbians, and most adult ones, practice it anywhere from occasionally to very often.[75] As with male gays, most of these lesbians both give and receive cunnilingus, and sometimes a couple will do it to each other at the same time (this, too, is known as "69").

Anal intercourse, or sodomy: This is the technique in

which a male inserts his penis into the anus of another person, female or male, and uses the anus as if it were a vagina.

In a few societies, it has been considered permissible for husbands to occasionally have anal intercourse with their wives for the sake of variety. In many others, it has been considered permissible for young boys or young men to use this technique with each other until they marry, and in a few others, as we have seen, for adult males to use it with their male "wives."[76]

In Europe, however, from the early centuries of Christianity onward, anal intercourse was considered the vilest of perversions, the blackest of sins. The same was true in America from the beginning of its colonization. But in recent years the sexual liberation movement has changed this ancient tradition somewhat. About half of the adults in the 1972 survey mentioned earlier said they did not think anal intercourse was wrong. But most of them avoided it: almost none of the people over thirty-five, and only about a quarter of the people under thirty-five, had ever experienced it, and very few had done so more than a few times.[77]

There are good reasons why most heterosexual couples do not find this a desirable sex technique, even if they have no feeling that it is wrong. For one thing, it is often painful for the woman. For another, it rarely leads to orgasm and satisfaction for her. Finally, because the rectum is an organ of elimination, there is always the risk of embarrassment and disgust.

But many homosexual men are willing to put up with these disadvantages, and anal intercourse is almost as widely used as fellatio. A large majority of male gays beyond their teens have anal intercourse anywhere from occasionally to very often.[78] Some prefer to be the one who enters, some prefer to be the one who is entered, but most male gays, whichever they prefer, actually do both. The one who enters always achieves orgasm; the one who is entered does so perhaps half the time, as the result of psychological excitement and stimulation of the prostate gland.[79]

Oddities and specialties: Certain odd or "kinky" sexual techniques are supposed to have particular appeal to homosexuals and to be more widely used by them than by heterosexuals. These sexual practices are often shown in pornographic movies, described in pornographic literature, and mentioned in advertisements in gay magazines. From such sources, you might easily get the idea that these techniques are very widely used. But the sex surveys and studies made in recent years show that most kinky sexual techniques are used by relatively few gay people, and are of little importance in understanding homosexuality. The odd or special sex techniques mentioned most often are:

The use of dildoes (artificial penises): Lesbians are widely believed to use them on each other, but only a minority ever do so, and for almost none of them is this their favorite sexual technique.[80]

S/M (sadomasochism): In S/M, one partner (the sadist) hits, whips, or in some way physically hurts the other (the masochist), and this causes them both to become sexually excited. There is a lot of trashy literature about S/M between straight people as well as gays. But people must like to read about it more than they like to do it; researchers say that it is rare among both straights and gays.[81]

Fetishism: Some straights and some gays cannot enjoy sex unless their partner is wearing certain items of clothing. Many sadomasochists, for instance, are strongly aroused by leather clothing—on themselves as well as on their partner—and some can only perform when one or both are wearing it. Some straight men cannot be aroused unless the woman is wearing black stockings and high heels, or other "sexy" items. Male gays are supposed to quite commonly have such special sexual needs, known as fetishes. But with most gay fetishists, it's just an amusing game, not a real sexual need. Anyway, even the game players seem to be a very small minority.[82]

Group sex: This is sexual activity involving a number of people who either take turns with one another or take part at the same time. Unlike the other specialties, this is fairly common among male homosexuals, according to some researchers. One recent study reported that over one quarter of the male gays in its sample had taken part in group sex, although most had done so only a few times.[83] In contrast to the male homosexuals, only a small number of straight men and women have ever tried group sex, and a great majority of these have done so only a few times. Very few lesbians ever take part in group sex.[84]

Roles: Who does what?

Straight people, in trying to understand what homosexuals do, naturally assume that in a sexual situation one gay person plays the masculine role and the other plays the feminine role. And in much writing about homosexuality, one does find the terms "active role" and "passive role" used as if they refer to the male and female roles in heterosexual sex. The same is true of several other pairs of terms, including "dominant" and "submissive," "butch" and "femme," and "master" and "slave."

There are two things wrong with these labels. The first is that they are often rather misleading as to who is doing what. It's true that in anal intercourse the male who enters is more active physically than the one who is entered. But in fellatio the one who "does" the other with his mouth is the more active physically—yet gays refer to his role as passive because he is entered.

For this reason, many sex researchers now use the terms "insertor" and "insertee." Whether the subject is fellatio, cunnilingus, or anal intercourse, and whether they are talking about male gays or lesbians, this makes it clear who is doing what.

In reading or listening to discussions of homosexuality, you can make things clear for yourself by simply translating terms in this way. If you read that a certain butch male gay or a butch lesbian insists on the active or dominant or master role, it means that he or she insists on being the insertor, whatever the technique being used. If you read that a certain nellie or femme wants only to play the passive or submissive or slave role, it means that he or she wants to be the insertee.

These roles do have a relationship to basic heterosexual behavior. In many species of animals, the male is aggressive and active, and the female submits, allowing herself to be mounted and entered. Likewise, in human lovemaking it used to be that the woman waited to be approached, and was expected to submit quietly and lie still while the man did what he did. But that's the second thing that's wrong with the labels for homosexual roles—they're somewhat out of date, because today we're not like that. Today few men expect a woman always to wait for their approach, or to submit if she doesn't want to, or to lie still during sex.

The male gays and the lesbians who insist on acting sexually as if they were persons of the other sex are driven by special emotional problems. The nellie may have a psychological need to be like a woman or a fear of being a man, and may therefore always seek to be the insertee, since this is closer to the female role. The butch lesbian may have a psychological need to be manly or a fear of being a woman, and may therefore insist on dominating her partner and being the insertor. One femme lesbian, describing her partner, says, "She makes love to me with a caring and concentration and gladness I've never experienced before. But she has her butch identity to protect, so that she does not want me to make love to *her*."[85]

Similarly, there are certain extra-tough supermasculine men, often called "rough trade," who maintain that they're straight but will indulge in fellatio or anal intercourse as long as they play the insertor role. In prison, stronger and tougher males often rape weaker, more timid ones; the tough ones are always insertors and are considered very manly. They are known as gorillas or jockers, while their victims are sneered at and called punks or girls. In female prisons, butch lesbians are called bulls or studs, and are always insertors to the femmes or "bitches" they dominate.

But most male gays and most lesbians are not this

rigid in their choice of sexual roles. It's still true that in gay bars many of the homosexual men and lesbians dress and behave so as to identify themselves as butch or femme. It's still true that in making a pickup gays often sound each other out as to sexual preferences, to make sure they can get what they want. It's still true that a fair number of gays prefer to be insertors, and a fair number of others prefer to be insertees. But the majority of male gays and lesbians like both roles; and many of those who prefer one role to the other are willing to play the less-preferred role, even in a casual relationship, in order to please their partner, so that in return their partner will please them.[86]

So when you see a homosexual couple and find yourself wondering who does what, the answer may not be as simple as you think. If one is definitely butch and the other definitely nellie or femme, there's a good chance that the butch is the insertor and the nellie or femme the insertee. But most homosexuals aren't clear-cut butches, or nellies, or femmes, and most of them don't cling to one sexual role. Like the majority of modern heterosexuals, they take turns starting things, are sometimes aggressive and sometimes yielding, will sometimes play one role and sometimes another, and at other times will play both.

How satisfactory is homosexual sex?

Both straights and gays often wonder how homosexual sex compares with heterosexual sex, and which is more satisfying. But it's a question that can never be answered.

When you say something tastes good or tastes bad, you are describing how it tastes to you; it may taste very different to someone else. When you and another person both say you are happy, there is no way to know whether what each of you feels is as strong as what the other feels. The same thing is true of sexual satisfaction. It's clear enough that gays find gay sex better for them than straight sex, but there's no way to know whether the satisfaction gays get from gay sex is less than or greater than the satisfaction straights get from straight sex. The two things are subjective—they're inside us, like happiness—and there's no way to measure them against each other.

That doesn't stop some of the more extreme gay activists from claiming that gay sex is basically better than straight sex. One male gay psychologist, for instance, makes this claim:[87]

> Homosexual experiences are generally characterized by attributes that are not so prevalent in heterosexual sex. Perhaps the major attribute is mutual concern and respect of the partners for each other. A homosexual couple in bed may do as well as, or even better than, a heterosexual couple. A gay man knows what feels good to his partner because he knows what makes his own body feel good.

And a well-known lesbian writer says much the same thing:[88]

> Not only is the psychic-emotional potential for satisfaction with another woman far greater than that with a man, but there is more likelihood of sexual fulfillment since all

organisms best understand the basic equipment of another organism which more closely resembles themselves.

In many articles, books, and rap sessions, male gays and lesbians have said not just that *they* find gay sex far better than straight sex but that *anyone* who gave it a fair try would have to agree.

That's the current party line—the up-to-date position of the militant gays. But for a number of reasons it isn't very convincing. For instance:

—Only a few years ago many gays were saying just the opposite. Donald Webster Cory, the most respected gay writer about gay life in the 1950's, had this to say: "Whatever form the physical expression may take, the sexual act is more likely to be frustrating for homosexuals, even for those who reach a climax, than a heterosexual act is for heterosexuals." This was so, he held, for two reasons: (1) the lack of a good physical fit, and (2) the fact that many homosexuals are not *looking for* a relationship so much as *running away* from the heterosexuality they fear.

—The homosexuality of hustlers and their johns, and of rough trade and their partners, is hostile, mechanical, and lacking in any personal warmth. So is most of the quick homosexual sex in restrooms, parks, and other public places.

—Many lesbians have admitted that tenderness and affection are what they want more than intense sexual experience and orgasm. This can be taken as an indication that these women do not get intense sexual satisfaction from lesbian sex. Similarly, one sociologist reports that a number of the male homosexuals he has interviewed want "friendship," and let themselves be used, sexually, to get it; the sex itself isn't important to them.[89]

—Some sex researchers have reported that homosexual men have more sexual problems than straight men, particularly in the areas of finding suitable partners and of sexual adequacy.[90]

—Finally, despite all the talk about sex among gays, gay men and women do *not* have more sex than straight men and women. Indeed, as we saw in Chapter 1, the opposite is the case. It's true that "hard-core" homosexuals who are deeply involved in the cruising, promiscuous life (which we'll look at it Chapter 7) have high rates of sexual activity. But broader samples of homosexual men have shown that in general they average fewer sexual experiences than straight men. Lesbians, too, taken as an overall group, tend to have somewhat fewer sex experiences than straight women.[91]

Despite all this, no one can argue with the gay people who say that they find gay sex intense and deeply satisfying. If they find it that way, then it *is* that way—for them. There's no point in trying to decide whether it's not as good, or just as good, or better than, straight sex. As the ancient Romans said, *De gustibus non est disputandum*—"There's no arguing about taste." If you like it, you like it; if the other person likes something else better, he likes it better. Straights can safely assume that most gays like what they're doing better than they would straight sex. And gays can (and should) assume that most straights like what they're doing better than they would gay sex.

5

THE FORK IN THE ROAD: GOING STRAIGHT OR GOING GAY

When do you know? What are the signs?

At what point in life do you know whether you're straight or gay? What are the telltale signs, what is the evidence, that you're one thing or the other?

These are questions that greatly trouble many young people from time to time during their early teen years. Some straights worry even into their twenties, thirties, and forties that they may really be homosexuals at heart. (Even those who aren't aware of such doubts may have them unconsciously; a straight young man or woman who has a homosexual dream, for instance, is usually rather upset by it without knowing why.) And some homosexuals refuse for many years to accept the evidence provided by their desires and reactions, and desperately keep trying to act and feel straight.

Sooner or later, most of these uncertain, anxious people

arrive at a fork in the road—a time when they finally recognize what their true feelings are and knowingly go one way or the other. But until they reach that fork, they wonder and worry about things like this:

—If a boy is delicate in build, and prefers reading and sewing to football and tree climbing, does that mean he's a "queer"? If he's no good at fighting, and gets along better with girls than with other boys, is he bound to grow up gay?

—If a girl is husky and strong, and prefers boys and ball games to girls and playing with dolls, does that mean she's not a "normal" girl? If she's an all-around tomboy, is she going to grow up lesbian?

—If two boys, at puberty, masturbate each other or make other sexual experiments, have they taken the gay fork in the road? Are they homosexuals at heart, even if they stop doing these things after a few months and never do them again?

—If two girls, at puberty, kiss each other and fondle each other's body, does that mean they're lesbians? Would it just be a waste of effort for them to try to be straight?

Most people think there are simple yes-or-no answers to these and similar questions—and that the answers are yes to all the ones above. But as we've seen, homosexuality isn't a single pattern of personality and behavior. It's many different patterns with many different causes, and therefore the "telltale signs" described above don't always tell the same tale; they don't necessarily indicate a homosexual future. And the other way around: some people who later turn out to be gay show no signs of it during childhood or puberty. You can't be certain ahead of time how or when a person will arrive at the fork in the road, or which way he or she will go. Young people become either straight or gay at different times in life, and in different ways.

Let's consider some of the ways in which people arrive at the fork in the road, and how they decide which path to take. We'll start early in the journey.

Sissies and tomboys

Most people believe that sissies and tomboys generally grow up to be gay, and that all gays must have been sissies or tomboys in childhood. Until recently, many gays thought so, too. But today social scientists know that many homosexual men are very masculine and always have been, and many homosexual women are very feminine and always have been. So the sissy-tomboy theory can't be right, at least not as far as these people are concerned.

But it isn't completely wrong, either. In one recent survey, two thirds of the gay men who were interviewed said that they had, indeed, been sissies during childhood, and more than two thirds of the lesbians interviewed said they had been tomboys.[92] Of course, what we mean by sissy or tomboy is changing these days; most people no longer think a boy peculiar if he likes to cook as long as he also likes climbing trees, and no longer think a girl peculiar if she likes to use carpenter's tools as long as she also likes dolls or other traditionally girlish toys. But, even by today's standards, the gay men and women in this survey would have been unusual children: the sissies hadn't had boy playmates or liked the usual boys' games but preferred girl playmates and girls' play activities; the tomboys hadn't had girl playmates or liked girls' play activities but preferred boys and boys' games. But that only proves that many homosexuals, when they were children, didn't act like other children of their own sex; it doesn't prove that all "different" children are bound to become homosexuals. That would be as illogical as saying that because all college students went to high school first, all people who go to high school will go to college.

In fact, many sissies do grow up straight. Most of them, as adults, continue to have interests and attitudes that are not typically "masculine" in the traditional, old-fashioned sense. Psychological tests show that heterosexual men in certain professions—ministers, musicians, and writers, for instance—have "feminine" attitudes toward sports, food, art, and animals. But some homosexual men are as "masculine" about such things as the straightest of straight truck drivers, policemen, and hard hats.[93]

The same is true of tomboys. Nearly three quarters of the lesbians in one study said they had been tomboys, but nearly half of the straight women in the same study had also been tomboys and didn't grow up gay.[94] And in psychological tests, women can show very "masculine" or very "feminine" attitudes, depending on their work and education, quite apart from whether they're straight or gay.[95]

Certainly, some sissies and tomboys do have strong homosexual tendencies even in childhood. But many others don't—they just have unusual personalities or tastes. Or, perhaps, atypical bodies: some boys are frailer, more delicate than we expect boys to be, some girls are sturdier and more muscular than we expect girls to be. What turns some of these children into homosexuals is the way people around them react to them. If a boy's classmates decide, for some reason, that he's a "queer," they will treat him like one; as the social scientists say, they *label* him gay. And being labeled may make a person behave the way he's expected to, because it's hard not to believe what everybody else says about him.[96] A boy who is called "queer" during childhood and treated as one may come to think he must be one; in his teens, there's a real chance he'll finally do what everybody, including himself, expects him to do. Here is how one homosexual man recalls his childhood:[97]

> I was called sissy and mama's boy. I was pushed and beaten by other boys. Boys would say "Eat me!"—meaning, Have sex with me. I was expected to be born a girl and my family constantly used a girl's name on me.

Is it any wonder that he grew up gay? How could he have believed himself anything else?

Many a tomboy, too, isn't basically homosexual until she begins to hear that people think she's peculiar and "not a real girl." The more she hears it, the more she believes it, and when the time comes for her to have sexual feelings and first crushes, there's a real chance she'll have them for other females, just as everyone, including herself, expects her to.

Summing up: Many sissies and tomboys are different from other boys and girls only in their body builds and in the activities they prefer. Most of these boys and girls grow up straight. But some others, though they do not have strong homosexual tendencies, if any, do become homosexual because their families and schoolmates label them as queer, treat them as queer, and all but force them to think of themselves that way and to look for friendship and comfort among gays.

Early sex experiences and "crushes"

We have already seen that most human beings, at birth, are capable of growing up homosexual, and that the reason most of us don't is that we are taught to be heterosexual. From early childhood on, we learn to think and feel heterosexually, and by the time we're adults most of us cannot imagine having sexual or romantic feelings about someone of our own sex. Most homosexuals, on the other hand, have learned a very different lesson as they were growing up, and as adults they are not sexually or romantically drawn toward persons of the opposite sex.

But those are the end results. During childhood and even the teens, many future straights and most future gays haven't yet come to the fork in the road. They aren't yet certain which they are, and without any clear intention to do so, they make experiments in both directions.

So do many of the higher animals. During the growing-up period, they attempt to have sex with playmates of their own sex as well as with those of the opposite sex.

But practically 100 percent of them come to prefer partners of the opposite sex; that's because animals are less flexible, and more ruled by inborn ways of acting, than human beings.[98]

In somewhat the same way, before adolescence many boys and girls play little sexual games ("doctor," "nurse") with playmates of both sexes. What is more important, in adolescence and the teens—when sex is no longer just a game—many future straights and most future gays experiment with persons of both sexes. Everyone knows, of course, about the heterosexual experiments of children and of teen-age boys and girls, but what isn't nearly so well known is the amount of homosexual experimenting they also do.

Before puberty, about half of all boys do some unimportant "fooling around" with other boys. And during puberty and the early teens, when their sex organs develop and fooling around seems much more important, about a quarter to a third of all boys have some homosexual experiences.[99] But most of them do so only a few times or for a very short period—a few weeks or months. Then they stop, partly because of guilt and fear, but largely because it doesn't "feel right" to them, although heterosexual activity does. Most of them then shut off and "forget" any homosexual feelings they may have had and become completely straight. Here's how one middle-aged man—who hasn't forgotten—recalls the homosexual experiments of his youth:

At twelve, my closest friend and I both discovered masturbation, and had contests to see who could do it fastest.

Then from a couple of dirty magazines we found out what it is that men and women do. We wanted to know what that was like, and decided to try it on each other—at least, that was our excuse. So we got undressed and tried to imitate intercourse, as nearly as possible. I can still remember how my heart pounded with excitement, but afterwards I felt terrible—kind of sick, inside, and disgusted by it all. But a few days later I wanted to do it again, and we did—and afterwards I felt even worse. He felt bad, too. After five or six times, without saying a word to each other, we just stopped doing it. For a while, we avoided each other, but after we began going out with girls, we became good friends again.

Much the same thing happens to many girls who later grow up straight. About a third of all girls play childish sex games with each other even before puberty. During puberty and the early teens, about the same number have homosexual experiences that are a good deal more intense, but most of them abruptly stop this same-sex activity after only one or a few times and lose all interest in it thereafter.[100] One straight woman remembers her adolescent homosexual experiments as follows:[101]

My first real sexual experience, at around eleven or twelve, was with my best friend. We started out by saying we had to practice up on kissing so we'd be ready for it when we started to date. So we kissed, and it got very exciting, and after a while we said, "What do they do next?" and took turns pretending that one of us was a boy, and feeling the other one up. Finally we were fingering each other's parts, and all of a sudden I had an orgasm. I was petrified. I was scared to death. I didn't know what it was, but I knew it was something very big and important, and that it was very wrong to have it with my best friend. So I never let it happen again. Until I began having sex with boys I often worried about having done it, but then that put an end to the worry. It has never interested me since except in fiction or sometimes the movies.

So much for the people who eventually grow up straight. How about those who eventually become gay? It's harder for them to accept the truth than it is for straights, because they know or feel in their bones that their preference is considered "abnormal" and shameful by most of the people around them. But their homosexual desires are strong and persistent. Most of the boys who later become gay have definite sexual feelings about other boys even in childhood, and in their early teens they begin having actual homosexual experiences fairly regularly.[102] Generally, they feel terribly guilty and are afraid of being found out by their parents, but that doesn't stop them.

But most of them don't yet think of themselves as gay. They're interested in girls; they take girls out, have crushes on them, and do some necking and petting. About half even have intercourse with a female sooner or later.[103] (Only about one out of every four gay men has never had any interest in or sexual feeling about girls.[104]) Even though these future gays are far more excited by males than by females, they either don't admit it to themselves or they tell themselves that they'll "grow out of it" or "just haven't met the right girl yet."

Some of the girls who grow up gay begin their homosexual sex experiences early, but the majority don't start until their middle or late teens, and some not until their twenties. Most of them, however, have unusually intense teen-age crushes on other girls, women teachers, and other women in their lives, though they rarely realize that these are homosexual feelings.[105]

At the same time, nearly all of them date during their teens, though some of them feel ill at ease with boys. Most of these future lesbians neck or pet with boys, and sooner or later at least half of them try intercourse.[106] During this long testing period, girls and women appeal to them far more strongly than men, both sexually and romantically, but they keep trying to ignore or deny their feelings. As one lesbian recalls:

> I was in my mid-teens when I first noticed that I found it more exciting to look at women's bodies in magazines, or on the beach, than at men's. I would see some well-built girl in a bathing suit, and stare at her, and imagine myself kissing her and fondling her all over, and I'd feel very sexually excited, much more so than I had ever been with any boy. When I was eighteen, and in college, I became very close to my roommate. We were really very warm and together. She'd walk around the room in the nude, and I would practically faint, I wanted so badly to hold and kiss her. And I would look away, and tell myself that I wasn't gay, I *wasn't!*

That last remark is the important one. Unlike the straights—who recognize their preference early and are glad to take the heterosexual path—most young men and women who eventually become gay fight against it for a long while, keep testing, and tell themselves that they're not really gay.

Trying not to be gay

Most of those who fight against becoming gay don't realize, for years, what they're doing. They're unaware, or only half-aware, of what is happening inside themselves. They go to all sorts of trouble to convince themselves that they're heterosexual or, at least, bisexual. Even though they have definite homosexual desires and homosexual experiences, they refuse to think of themselves as gay or to become part of gay society. Here are some of the ways in which they keep up the fight:

—Until their late teens or early twenties, most future gays continue to date people of the opposite sex and to have romantic feelings about some of them and physical contact with them.[107]

—Some future gays permit themselves to have homosexual sex only when they're drunk; they tell themselves afterward that they didn't know what they were doing. (The next day they'll even say such things as, "Boy, was I drunk last night! I can't remember a thing.") Others have homosexual sex only if they're asleep when the first moves are made by a friend or roommate; they tell themselves afterward that they didn't realize what was happening.[108]

—Many future gays rely on mental tricks rather than on alcohol or sleep. They deny, they make excuses, they give other names to their homosexual activities ("just fooling around"), all to deceive themselves as much as other people. Psychologist Evelyn Hooker interviewed one man who ran a club for gay men, and who lived with one and often had sex with him—but who insisted that he himself wasn't gay. The club, he said, was just business; as for his living with a gay man and having sex with him, that didn't mean a thing, because he'd had sex with women, too, and was still thinking about getting married some day.

—Others, trying to run away from their homosexual feelings, make special efforts to have sex with persons of the opposite sex, as if this will "save" them or change them. One young woman said that she "went through about twenty-five men" in a year, when she was nineteen, trying to prove to herself that she was straight. But most of the time she would picture lesbian sex acts to herself while some man was making love to her. Only later did she say, "I don't know why it wasn't clear to me what the real story was."

—Even when future gays can't deny the evidence of their daydreams, nighttime dreams, and sex experiences, they may cling to any popular belief, any bit of "folk wisdom," that allows them to hope that they're not really gay. One premed student was so horrified and depressed by his homosexual tendencies that he went to see a psychiatrist. The psychiatrist, who wasn't any too well informed, said, "Well, you can't be a homosexual, because you want to go to medical school. Homosexuals don't want to be doctors. If you were a homosexual, you'd want to be a beautician or something." Years later, the student

—by then a doctor, and thoroughly gay—said, "Strange as it may seem, that reassured me. So I went to medical school and sort of said, mentally, 'I'm not.' "[109]

—Some future gays manage to fool themselves by having only the most impersonal kind of sex relations with people of their own sex. One young man had hundreds of homosexual experiences with strangers in public toilets, over a period of years, but because he and his partners never spoke to each other, he didn't think of this activity as involving his real self. He didn't consider himself a homosexual because all of his social relationships were with women.

—Some gays get married, hoping that doing so will "straighten them out." But many of these marriages soon break up, and the gay-inclined person gives up the struggle against homosexuality. Others remain married but continue to have homosexual sex on the outside. Men and women who do this usually tell themselves that they're really straight or mostly straight (after all, they *are* married, aren't they?), and that the outside experiences are "just a little something extra." In America today, at least a million married women and two to three million married men have homosexual experiences outside their marriages, but most of these people don't think of themselves as homosexuals.[110]

Coming out

Sooner or later, most gays face the truth. At some point, they admit to themselves that they're homosexual and from then on think about themselves that way. It happens to a few as early as childhood, and to a few as late as middle age. It happens to some before they have had any homosexual sex experiences, and to others only after many years of having such experiences. But on the average, for males the moment of self-recognition comes in the late teens, after about four to six years of homosexual feelings and sex experiences. For females, on the average, it comes a little later.[111]

Gays call this "coming out." Actually, the expression has two meanings. The first is the recognition, within one's self, that one is a homosexual; the other is the first visit a gay person makes to a public place where homosexuals meet and where he or she becomes for the first time part of homosexual society.

The recognition of one's homosexuality may seem to come as a surprise, but usually the person has been unconsciously preparing for it. Little by little, he or she has been adopting a new view of homosexuals and discarding most of the harsh attitudes toward them that he or she learned while growing up. Then one day some bit of conversation or some small action flips the switch and casts a new light on the real self.[112]

One young man told a sociologist that although he'd been having sex with other males for years, he thought of it only as something that felt good. "That's as far as it went," he said. "But I never would have thought of kissing a man on the mouth. When I finally did kiss a guy romantically, I realized that I was a homosexual."[113]

A young woman had had sex experiences with both men and women but never thought of herself as a lesbian; she simply thought herself a rather liberated person. Then she fell deeply in love with another young woman and they had a steady relationship. One day, after they'd been a couple for six months, her female lover asked her, "Are you always going to be a lesbian?" She was astonished. A *lesbian?* And as if this had never occurred to her before, she thought, Well, I guess this *does* make me a lesbian.[114]

Most often, however, the switch is flipped by the person's first introduction to homosexual society; coming out in the first sense is caused by coming out in the second sense. A gay man who isn't fully aware of his own gayness may for the first time wander into a gay bar or be taken by a friend to a gay party, and suddenly realize that he is one of these people, that he has found his own kind.

Sometimes, to be sure, the first look at gay society is frightening. The young woman quoted above, after she realized the truth about herself, went with her lover to a lesbian bar to see what other lesbians were like. Within a few minutes, she was approached by a pipe-smoking bull dyke who, in a tough, super-butch tone of voice, asked her to dance; this view of lesbianism alarmed her, and she left as fast as she could.

Far more often, the first view of gay society is exciting and reassuring. It brings about a kind of conversion, a surrender to one's real feelings and a resulting sense of relief. This is the way it seemed to a man of twenty-three who had been having homosexual experiences for many years but had never been able to admit to himself that he was gay:[115]

I knew that there were homosexuals, queers, and what not; I had read some books, and I was resigned to the fact

that I was a foul, dirty person, but I wasn't actually calling myself a homosexual yet. [But] the time I caught myself coming out is the time I walked into this bar and saw
a whole crowd of groovy, groovy guys. And I said to myself
that not all gay men are dirty old men or idiots, silly
queens. I saw gay society, and I said, "Wow, I'm home."
That night in the bar saved my sanity.

Coming out makes life easier, emotionally, for the gay
person. He or she no longer feels alone; there are others
of the same kind, there is a whole world he or she can fit
into. And coming out ends the battle within, the ex-
hausting effort to pretend, to deny, to choke back the
gay desires, to force oneself to act like a heterosexual. According to a team of sociologists at Indiana University,
gays who have come out are psychologically healthier
than those who haven't: they like themselves better, they
have fewer symptoms of anxiety, and they are less depressed.[116] In fact, after coming out, only a minority of
gay men and gay women wish they could give up their
homosexuality and be straight.[117]

But despite these psychological benefits, coming out
has its problems. To the newcomer, the gay world is like
a foreign country. It has its own words, its own gestures,
and its own customs, and he or she can easily feel awkward and ignorant, or get into bad situations by not
knowing the signals.

In some cities, gay men who wear a bunch of keys
dangling over the left hip are notifying other gays that
they are sexually dominant (insertors). A newcomer who
doesn't know this and goes home with such a person may

have an unpleasant or even physically violent encounter. A newcomer to the lesbian world may be treated as a femme because she is wearing a scarf, or as a butch because she is wearing boots; if she doesn't know about the local signals, she may be in for some harsh words.

Novices have to learn about rough trade, police raids, teen-age "queer-baiters" who beat up gays, straight sightseers who come to look and laugh.

Some newcomers enjoy their freedom to swish in the gay world, but they have to learn to switch off the new voice and the new movements when it's time to go back home, or to work or to school. They have to live like spies, keeping their "cover" in place and never letting the truth slip out when they're among straights. For coming out doesn't necessarily mean coming out of the closet; that's an even bigger step, one that most gays never take.

Coming out of the closet

Coming out of the closet would seem to be the final step in coming out. After learning at last to accept oneself as a homosexual, the gay person would like above all else to be accepted in the same way by the straight world—by parents, brothers and sisters, friends, neighbors, employers, co-workers. Accepted as gay, but as an equal; different, yes, but equal.

To come out of the closet, to give up hiding, pretending, and lying, to no longer fear being exposed, is the dream of many gays. But it seems an impossible dream to most of them. The gay liberationists and others who have been able to come out of the closet are still a small minority. But the great majority of gays feel that for themselves the cost of coming out of the closet would greatly outweigh the benefits. And in general they are still right.

For in most parts of America, to be known as gay is to be stigmatized—that is, to live like a person with a visible mark of disgrace that all the world can see. In earlier centuries, in other countries, a thief might have his nose or hand cut off to mark him as a worthless person. Never could he walk down the street without being stared at in scorn. Nowhere would he be treated as the equal of other men. And for a gay to come out in the open, even today, is somewhat like that. Whether the gay person comes out of the closet deliberately, or whether his secret is revealed by accident, he or she is no longer just another person, but a gay person, a marked person.

In Chapter 3 we saw what that can mean. First and worst, it can often mean being rejected, with disgust and anger, by one's own parents. In the autobiographical writings of many gays, the moment of telling their mother or father seems to have been the hardest part of coming out of the closet. Brothers and sisters, too, sometimes react with shock and avoid the gay from then on.

Oliver Sipple, an ex-Marine, saved President Ford's life during an assassination attempt in San Francisco in 1975. It made Sipple famous; it also led to newspaper reports that he was a member of the local homosexual community. Sipple's parents, brothers, and sisters, who hadn't known about his homosexuality, promptly stopped speaking to him.

Even when families aren't repelled, they may avoid the gay person for social reasons. One gay writer says that since he came out of the closet, his parents do not mention him to some of their friends, for fear of losing them. And when one lesbian told her parents about herself, they said, in effect, "We still love you, but of course we won't be able to see you any more. Drop us a line now and then so we'll know you're still alive."

Straight friends, too, no matter how long-standing and dear they are, may become uncomfortable with the gay person who has come out of the closet. If they are unmarried, they will probably stop seeing the gay for fear of being thought to be gay themselves.

In many parts of America, gays who come out of the closet run the risk of being demoted or fired, or of being rejected for jobs they are fully qualified for. This can happen if they are exposed by some blackmailer or by a police raid on a gay bar, but it can also happen if they tell the world about themselves in order to try to live openly and honestly.

Take the case of Air Force Sergeant Leonard Matlovich. In 1975, after twelve years in the service, a perfect record, and medals for bravery and for being wounded in Vietnam, he told his commanding officer that he was a homosexual. Because he had been a very good soldier, he thought he could break down the rule against homosexuals in the service. But the five officers presiding at his court-martial paid no attention to his good character and fine record. He said he was gay— and that was all they needed to know; they threw him out of the Air Force.

When Elaine Noble, the lesbian who is now in the Massachusetts legislature, first came out of the closet, she paid dearly for it. She lost her job, lost her lover (who was afraid to be seen with her), got nasty telephone calls, and found obscene words written on her car and her tires slashed. She said later that she felt for a while as if she had lost part of her sanity.

It's true that things are changing, and that many of the gays who have come out of the closet find that they can survive pretty well among straights who know about them. The penalties, they say, are not as bad as they had feared—and definitely not as bad as the penalties of living in secrecy, with the constant fear of being exposed. But this doesn't mean that coming out of the closet is the best move for all homosexuals in all parts of America. Whether it is or not depends on the kind of community they live in, the kind of work they do, and the kind of people they have for family and friends. For most gays, the chance that coming out of the closet would ruin their lives is still too great to take.

Bisexuality

Not all straights and gays choose one road and follow it the rest of their lives. Some gay men in their thirties and forties find that they're getting too old to make out well in gay bars, and give up the gay life and get married. And some married people, after many years of being straight, finally give in to desires they had been bottling up and turn gay.[118]

But there are still others who spend many years, or even their whole lives, switching back and forth between male partners and female partners, between acting straight and acting gay. They think of themselves as bisexuals, people who can love and have sex with partners of either sex. In a few cities and on a few college campuses, bisexuality is something of a fad these days. Certain rock stars and performers who are much admired by young people have publicly discussed their own bisexuality (David Bowie is one, Joan Baez another). Those who favor bisexuality claim that it's freer and more natural than being completely straight or completely gay. We'd all be bisexual, they say, if we weren't afraid to be, or hadn't been taught not to be. Some sex researchers agree with them.

But for all the talk, there aren't many bisexuals around. For one thing, they aren't very popular with anybody but other bisexuals. Most straights, gays, and sex researchers say that nearly all bisexuals are merely homosexuals who aren't willing to admit that they're really gay.[119] Gays don't trust people who keep a toehold in the straight world; lesbians in particular feel that a bisexual woman would easily leave a female lover for a man. And straights are very uneasy and mistrustful in a sex or love relationship with someone who has had, or is still having, homosexual experiences.

For another thing, in our world it's almost impossible to be a true bisexual. The complicated sexual and emotional feelings, learned during childhood and the teens, that cause us to be attracted to another human being run too deep to be easily switched back and forth. A man who has been trained to love women isn't geared to respond to another man. A woman who has learned to love men isn't prepared to respond to another woman. We could, perhaps, be trained to do both, but it would take a total revolution in the way parents raise their children, and there aren't any signs of such a revolution in the offing.

For the time being, those who can shift from straight relationships to gay ones and back again seem to be persons who don't get emotionally involved, who don't relate to a whole human being but focus their attention only on one thing—a sexual organ, or a particular sensation.[120] "It's like apples and oranges," says one bisexual man, "I like them both." But human beings aren't apples or oranges, and a man who treats them as if they were is not letting himself have real relationships.

Some bisexuals do have deeper relationships—but not with both sexes. There are men, for instance, who are married, and seem to have genuine relationships with their wives, but who slip out once a week for an hour or two of quick homosexual sex with some stranger.[121] There are women who do somewhat the same sort of thing. It's hard to know what to call them; perhaps they're homosexuals who haven't come out and who are forcing themselves to live a lie.

Aren't there any real bisexuals, then? Those who call themselves bisexuals say that there are. A few sociologists and psychiatrists agree. They say that women's liberation is breaking down the old water-tight, male-female compartments we used to live in and letting us become aware of the possibilities of loving persons of both sexes.

But most sex researchers have not found that sort of freedom in the bisexuals they have been studying. They find most of them to be shallow and emotionally undeveloped persons who jump back and forth chiefly because they don't and can't love anyone of either sex, or because they're afraid to commit themselves to one way of life or the other.[122]

It may be that at some time in the future, when we have become much more tolerant of homosexuality than we are now, it will seem natural to us to love persons of the same sex as well as of the other sex. This has sometimes been the case in other lands and in other times. But that future seems far off. For the present, true bisexuals are very few in number, and don't seem to be making many converts from either the straight world or the gay world.

6

HOMOSEXUAL

TASTE

"Do they know something we don't know?"

The place: a movie house in Chicago. Bette Davis is on the screen—aging, wrinkled, popeyed. She's playing the part of a mean old woman, and doing it with such exaggeration, such glaring, fidgeting, and face twitching, that you would expect people to walk out. But the audience, consisting mostly of gay men, loves it. They howl with laughter, they roar with delight. There are some straight people in the audience and they can't figure out what's going on. What the gays are enjoying so much is a mystery to them, and one straight whispers to another, "Do they know something we don't know?"

The place: the streets of San Francisco. A well-to-do man and his wife are spending the day going from store to store with their decorator in search of fabrics and furnishings for their new apartment. He takes them to a number of fine antique shops; most are run by gays. He takes them to a showroom where beautiful and unusual wallpapers may be specially ordered; it's run by a couple of gays. He takes them to two stores where handsome drapery materials are on display; one is run by a gay man and the other by a lesbian. Finally the man says to his wife, privately, "They seem to know something the rest of us don't know."

The place: a theater in New York City. The audience, which has come to see a new and experimental ballet, seems to be half gay, half straight. What's happening on stage doesn't look at all like what most people think of as ballet, for the dancers are striding, jumping, and tumbling about in odd, abrupt, almost violent ways, or else stay frozen in some peculiar position for minutes at a time. They don't dance together, and seem not even to see each other. Nor do they move in time to the music—which itself is very odd, being a series of tape-recorded peeps, deep organ tones, squeals, rumbles, thumps, and hisses. When the performance is over, the audience is of two minds about it: some people applaud politely or not at all, but others are enthusiastic and some even leap to their feet shouting bravos. One straight couple, baffled by the ballet, notice that many of the most enthusiastic members of the audience are gays. The man leans over to the woman and whispers, "What do they know that we don't know?"

It often seems to straight people that there is something special and different about the artistic taste of gays. Like other generalizations about gays, this one is true only of some of them, not of all. Many homosexual men and women have the same range of taste in music, dance, books, art, movies, clothing, and furnishings as straight people. Yet it is also true that a good many gays have special artistic tastes which are distinctly different from those of most straight people, and that gays have a special place in the artistic world. "Gay taste" isn't the taste of all gays, and perhaps not even of most of them; yet it is a real thing, a very noticeable thing—and, to many straights, a thoroughly puzzling thing.

Puzzling because it seems to be made up of opposites. A good many gays are admirers of certain kinds of acting, singing, music, art, and home decor that seem to most straights to be the purest junk. Yet gays are often "tastemakers" in the arts—they are among the first to understand and appreciate important new trends in painting, music, performing, and fashion, and they outnumber straights in some fields of artistic creation.

So straights don't know what to make of gay taste. Sometimes they think it's a put-on, a way of trying to act superior to the rest of the world. At other times they think it's real, and suspect that gays are more artistic and more sensitive than straights.

Which is right? In a sense, neither—because many homosexuals do not have any special or different kind of gay taste. But in a sense, both—because many other homosexuals do exhibit gay taste, and this is of two contradictory kinds. Many gays are definitely fond of *kitsch* (from a German word for "trash" or anything in bad taste). That's why certain groups of gays make a fuss over Bette Davis in her bad roles (the worse the better).

That's why they were the first and most enthusiastic admirers of the singer Bette Midler, who specializes in vulgarity (of which she is actually making fun). That's why they are noisy fans of certain foul-mouthed female comics. That's why they were among the first to support such "pop art" as a sculpture of a bag of groceries and paintings done in comic-strip style.

That's the kitsch side of gay taste. But there's another side. Fifty years ago, when most people were still sneering at Picasso and certain other modern painters, it was Gertrude Stein and Alice B. Toklas, the famous lesbian couple, who were their strongest supporters. Today, too, gays are often among the first to support important new kinds of art, writing, drama, and dance. Many of the most gifted stage designers and choreographers are gay; so are a number of the best-known playwrights, actors, singers, and musicians; so are many of the most original decorators and illustrators. Many of the leading designers of women's clothes are gay men—and now they're the top designers of men's clothes, too. And it's the gays in our population—some of them, anyway—who are usually the first to catch on to what's new in clothing fashions; they're generally two or three years ahead of the straight world. Many gays seem to dress better or more interestingly than straights, and decorate their own apartments or houses with unusual care and style.

So straights are doubly puzzled by gay taste. Why do gays so often like kitsch—and why, at the same time, are they so often the creators of, or the greatest admirers of, the newest and best in the arts and in fashion?

Are gays more creative than straights?

It is often said, mostly by gays themselves, that their taste is special and different because they are more creative—that is, they have more artistic talent—than straights. (For the most part, we mean male gays—not because lesbians are inherently less creative than male gays, but because throughout history, lesbians, like other women, have rarely had the time, the education, or the freedom to practice any of the arts. This chapter, therefore, deals chiefly with the artistic taste and talent of male gays.)

Gay militants never tire of listing the famous creative people who have been gay. They name such great writers of the past as Plato, Sappho, Francis Bacon, Swinburne, Walt Whitman, Oscar Wilde, Virginia Woolf, André Gide, Colette, and Marcel Proust, and they even claim Shakespeare, though there's no solid evidence in his case. These days, with more and more gays coming out of the closet, there are a number of living writers to add to the list: Christopher Isherwood, Edward Albee, Truman Capote, Allen Ginsberg, to name only a few. How about painters, sculptors, composers? Well, from the past there's Leonardo da Vinci, Michelangelo, Cellini, and Tchaikovsky, for a start; and among the living, the list would run half a page. But why go on? Putting it briefly, many gays and some sex researchers believe that the record shows gays to be, on the average, more artistic and creative than straights.[123] And this claim is made not just about those who actually create artistic works but about all those gays who appreciate important new works of art and who exercise good taste in their own choice of clothing and furnishings, for these people are artistic and creative in a general sense.

Yet you don't really prove anything by simply naming a lot of creative people who have been gay. If you could make a complete list of *all* creative people, and divide it into those who were gay and those who were straight, then you might prove something. But that's impossible, since so many gays have remained in the closet—and also since so many straights have been wrongly thought gay just because they were artistic.

There is, though, a scientific way to test the belief. You take a sample of gays, and for each gay find a straight of the same age, income, education, and background. Then you test both the gays and the straights for creativity. If gays are more often creative, the overall averages of their test scores should come out higher than the overall averages of the straights.

A few years ago a psychologist at Fordham University did just that. He collected 125 gay volunteers, and for each one found a matching straight volunteer. He then gave all of them nine different, well-known tests of creativity. (The volunteers did such things as complete an incomplete drawing, think up offbeat uses for an everyday object, like a brick, and so on.) When the psychologist scored all the tests, he found that most of them showed no difference between gays and straights. And, surprisingly, in those few tests which did show some difference, the straights scored higher in creativity than the gays.[124]

Another popular belief—that most gays work in artistic

professions—can also be scientifically tested, in this case by surveys. Researchers have surveyed samples of homosexuals as to what they do for a living; the results show that only a very small percentage are in artistic professions, while the vast majority are in business, sales, government, and other non-artistic kinds of work.[125]

But even if most gays aren't in the arts, it's still true that an unusual number of people in the arts are gay. Why is that so, if they don't have more talent than straights?

One explanation you're likely to hear is that male gays are drawn to things like ballet and decorating because these are "feminine" forms of activity and gays are feminine. There's something to that: many male gays, especially the sexually "passive" ones, show traditional feminine attitudes in psychological tests.[126] But ballet and decorating are feminine only in our American minds. In many other countries, these same activities are thought of as quite suitable for masculine men. In Russia, for instance, most of the great male dancers are straight. Anyway, this explanation doesn't tell us why there are so many gays in other arts, such as painting, sculpture, and classical music—none of which seems "feminine," even to Americans.

Another common explanation is that homosexuals don't create children, so they fulfill the reproductive urge by creating works of art. There may be something to that —it may be true that some people who don't have the satisfactions of family life may find substitute satisfactions in art. But it isn't a good enough explanation, because it explains only one part of the puzzle. It doesn't say why the vast majority of childless gays don't do anything creative, or why so many straight people have had children and have still been driven to create works of art. Remember Johann Sebastian Bach?—he was the father of twenty children, and one of the greatest composers in history.

But there is a broader and more convincing explanation of the high percentage of gays in the creative professions. Most sociologists who have studied the question say that gays tend to go where they are best accepted—and unusual or different people have always been better accepted in the arts than in other occupational areas. The general public, for instance, is still against letting homosexuals work in government and the schools, but thinks it's fine for them to be artists and performers.[127] In the arts, gays can be themselves, can come out of the closet; elsewhere in American life they have to stay in the closet to keep their jobs. So a talented person, if he or she is gay, has an even stronger pull toward the arts than a straight person with the same amount of talent. The artistic life, for a gay, is more than a way of earning a living, more than a way of expressing oneself. It's a way of living in relative freedom.

This helps explain why there are so many gays in artistic fields, but it doesn't explain why many gay artists (and many gays who are not artists) have unusual or special kinds of taste. Yet very often it seems as if they do, as if there's something *different* about their taste. And that's the key to answering the question "What do they know that we don't know?" The real question isn't why gay taste is better or gays are more creative, because it isn't and they aren't. The real question is: Why is gay taste *different?*

Gay originality

The first thing that's different about gay taste is that often it's highly *original* or *inventive*. This is as true in the "highbrow" arts as it is in popular arts, like pop music and fashion.

This is not to say that all gay artists are original, and it certainly doesn't mean that everything original in the arts is the work of gays. Still, it does seem true that many gays in the arts are unusually imaginative, daring, or iconoclastic, and that many of the wildest costumes of pop singers and the most offbeat ideas in fashion are the products of gay creativity.

But if gays aren't the only people in our society who can be original or imaginative, they may well have a stronger urge in this direction than most straights. There's a good reason for that. Most people get what they want out of life by doing what is expected of them, going along with the rules, and acting as they've been taught to act. They go to school, graduate, get jobs, do their work, and slowly advance to a certain level of success.

But what if outside obstacles get in the way? Some people can't get anywhere when they stick to the rules because they're handicapped by their race, their parents' poverty, their religion—or their homosexuality. Sociologists say that when people are held back by such impediments, and can't succeed in life by sticking to the rules, they tend to break the rules. Some just give up trying to get anywhere (that's breaking a "rule" in itself). Others become rebels and try to overthrow society. But many become "innovators"—they look for new or unusual ways of achieving success.

Innovation—you could also call it originality—doesn't mean being creative in just the arts. It can also mean thinking up a new way to rob a jewelry store or to pull off a swindle in the stock market, or founding a new religion, or dreaming up a new scheme to assassinate a President, or coming up with a new scientific theory. Those are all kinds of originality, though they're not all good kinds.

Of course, not all innovative people are creative because they have handicaps. Many of the world's innovative people have been reasonably fortunate and have not had to break the rules in order to succeed. They have been innovative for the sheer joy of it. But all things considered, the handicapped person has a *greater need* than other people to take chances, think new thoughts, devise new solutions to old problems.

One could fill a book with stories of successful artists, writers, and scientists who started out poor, were of lowly birth, or were deformed in some way. Their disadvantages were partly responsible for the originality of their work. Naturally, no one can become a Plato, a da Vinci, or a Michelangelo simply by trying hard to think daring new thoughts; you also have to have inborn genius. But at least some part of the originality of homosexual writers and artists is a response to their being at a disadvantage in society.

What about the great majority of gays, who are not in the arts? Many of them take chances in a different way—they are the earliest admirers of new styles, new art. Some people call them "faddists," but others more kindly call them "avant-garde," meaning they are front-runners or trend setters. This, too, is a kind of innovation, and comes from much the same need to succeed. Most homosexuals, as we have seen, have a poor opinion of themselves as they are growing up. But because it is painful to go through life this way, many of them learn to think better of homosexuality and of themselves.[128] One way they do this is to see themselves as having better taste than the people all around them—that's a kind of success.

This is why many gays seize on new trends in the arts and adopt the latest fashions before the straight world has done so. It gives them a feeling of being superior to the rest of society, of being more sensitive and tasteful. And it delights them that often the straight world first sneers at the new trend—and then adopts it. By that time, however, the gays think it's old hat and are onto something else.

Camp

Gay taste isn't always original and artistic. Much of the time, what's special about it is that it's hostile, in a funny, bitchy way. Many gays are particularly fond of a kind of art, fashion, and behavior that is mocking, sarcastic, or even nasty about femininity, masculinity, family life, parenthood, childhood, love, beauty, work—and even homosexuality. This style of art, fashion, and behavior goes by the name of "camp."

The words "camp" and "camping" first were used to mean gay male behavior of a deliberately super-swishy and humorous kind. If a gay man is somewhat effeminate by nature, that isn't camping, but if a gay man puts on an exaggerated and ridiculous feminine manner, that *is*. When gay men speak in lisping voices, bat their eyelashes at each other, mince around with limp-wristed, hip-wiggling movements, and call each other "Mary" and "Alice," that's camp. When a gay actor in a Broadway show plays the part of a gay man who flits around on tiptoe, throws tantrums, and bursts into tears whenever he's frustrated, that's camp. When gays come to a party gotten up as angels with wings or as peacocks with huge feathered tails, that's camp.

Gays, when they camp, aren't always just making fun of themselves; often they're being scornful of the straight world. Their takeoffs on feminine mannerisms and clothing show contempt for women, just as most jokes about Jews or blacks show contempt for them. And camping isn't always meant just for other gays to see and laugh at; sometimes it's meant to be seen by straights, to annoy them. Even gay women get into this act at times: lesbians who wear men's clothes and adopt a super-butch way of walking and talking are sometimes just camping to amuse themselves—but when they do so in public, it can be because they enjoy seeing the straights around them looking offended or shocked.

In the mid-1960's, camp became widely accepted as the name of a kind of art as well as a kind of behavior. It became the "in" thing with some gays to admire and praise all sorts of ugly, overdone kitsch; this is another way of mocking the straight world. These gays love a New York ballet troupe—Les Ballets Trockadero—in which tall, muscular men dressed as ballerinas dance the part of the delicate swans in *Swan Lake*; that's camp. They like sofas, lamps, sculptures, paintings that are especially vulgar and "tacky"; they're camp. At a recent party to publicize a new movie, the star of the movie— a fat man dressed as a woman, and known as "Divine"— wore a cheap blond wig and a blue bra-and-miniskirt cocktail dress, with his (her) huge naked belly hanging out; that's camp. Divine's movie was a comedy called *The Heartbreak of Psoriasis* (psoriasis is a serious skin disease); that's camp.

As one expert has put it, camp is the "love of the unnatural: of artifice and exaggeration." Or in the words of a gay writer, camp is "carefully cultivated vulgarity."

Why do many gays like camp art? For the same reason they like camp behavior—because it's a way of making fun of themselves, but also and more importantly, of the world around them. It's a way of mocking the effeminacy of nellie gays, but also a way of belittling feminine women and the straight men who find them appealing. It's a way of showing scorn for the straight world by admiring the worst it has produced—the trashiest movies, the ugliest furnishings, the most vulgar acting and singing, the lowest comedy.

In short, it's a way of getting even.

And the funniest part is that many straights, believing there's something special about all gay taste, have come to admire camp. They have mistaken it for gay taste at its most daring and original. They have been fooled into thinking that camp art is the new thing, the smart thing. They have been tricked into admiring their own junk. So now there is camp everywhere—in movies, in novels, in magazine advertising. It's camp produced by straights, for straights. Take just one example: *Young Frankenstein*, the latest movie about Dr. Frankenstein and his monster, was pure farce, and totally silly; you could never experience the least feeling of wonder, or fear, or pity, because the whole thing was a takeoff. That's camp conquering the straight world.

Camp itself may soon be conquered by gay liberation, in the sense of being made unnecessary and old-fashioned. Camp is a way of making fun of oneself for being homosexual, but gay militants say there's nothing to make fun of, that homosexuals can and should be self-respecting. Camp is also a way of thumbing one's nose at the straight world, but gay militants say thumbing one's nose isn't good enough; fighting for homosexual rights in the courts, the streets, and the news media is vastly more important. As a result, many younger gays, who grew up and came out after the gay liberation movement got under way, either are uninterested in camp or actively disapprove of it, much as today's blacks disapprove of "Uncle Tom" behavior toward whites.

Gay sensitivity

There's also a sensitive, suffering side to gay taste. To some extent, camp is this side in disguise—the grin that hides the pain inside.

Until recent years, many homosexuals were often unhappy or depressed. As society has become somewhat more tolerant of them, this has been changing, but even today, at least one out of every four gay men considers himself less happy than other people and often feels downcast and dejected.[129] Nearly half of gay men still feel, at times, as if they are going to have a nervous breakdown.[130] And even those who think themselves reasonably happy frequently have their dark moods, their bad times, because they still live as outsiders—either in secrecy, or out in the open but cut off from the rest of society. No wonder a recent book on how to enjoy the gay life devotes many of its pages to ways to fight "gay blues" and "gay fears."

For these reasons, many gays have a special fondness for the sad and the sentimental. That's why they still worship the memory of Judy Garland. Her life was a series of successes and failures and comebacks, of broken love affairs and marital problems, of battles against overweight, drugs, and greedy producers. When she sang, all her anxiety and heartbreak was in her face and voice; that's why gays loved her, and cheered and wept when she was on stage. That's why a gay writer says, of a new biography of Judy Garland, "It's the kind of book you can read and then have a good cry over."

A good many gays are fond of all kinds of art, whether highbrow or lowbrow, that have to do with misfortune and emotional suffering. Gays are among the weepiest and most appreciative people in the audience at the tragic ending of the ballet *Giselle* or of the opera *La Bohème*. At the same time they are among the most responsive fans of certain black pop singers; as a writer for *The Advocate*, a gay magazine, says: "Their emotional, high-pitched, screaming songs are favorites with gays because they reflect the despair and desperateness that often haunt the lives of homosexuals."

Gay elegance

Finally, there's another, very different side of gay taste—the gay love of elegant, refined, and "pretty" things, especially in home decor. It's the liking some gays have for velvet drapes, china figurines, dim lighting, chairs covered in needlepoint, Irish linen on the dinner table, bone china, crystal chandeliers. But this is not just gay taste, it's the taste of many straight women, the ones who read popular magazines like *Better Homes and Gardens* and *House Beautiful*.

Today, many gays—especially the more or less liberated ones—look down on this kind of taste. They consider it old-fashioned in gays, and an imitation of femininity. They say that gay men used to think they were rebelling against masculinity and expressing their own femininity by making things pretty, but that this is actually playing the part the straights want gays to play. It's putting themselves down. It's the taste, says gay writer Craig Alfred Hanson, of "bitchy male hairdressers, snobbish antique dealers, and effete ballet masters." These effeminate gays —or gay traditionalists—see themselves as the straights do: as women in men's bodies. So they outdo themselves in making things pretty. Liberated gays often sneer at them as "fairy princesses" and at their homes as "fairy palaces."

This kind of taste is elegant—but among liberated gays it's scornfully called "piss-elegant," to show contempt for it. There's nothing wrong with elegance, except that in the eyes of gay liberationists it's often an effort to win the admiration of the straight world by doing the "right" thing. As gay psychologist Mark Freedman puts it: "The right clothes, the right wallpaper, the right crystal and carpets, and engraved invitations—these things say implicitly that the person should be accepted and admired by society *even though he is a homosexual.*"

Gay taste of this kind can be, in short, a way of playing up to the straight world, being what the straights say it's all right for gays to be.

The end of gay taste

What do all these different kinds of gay taste have in common? One thing: they are all the results of the homosexual's position in society, of his being looked down on. (Lesbians, as we have seen, have never been as severely ostracized or condemned as male homosexuals; that, along with women's lack of education and opportunity during most of the past, probably explains why they have not developed taste as distinctively gay as that of gay men.)

All the characteristics of gay taste—originality, camp, sensitivity, and elegance—grow out of the gay's being discriminated against and looked down upon by straight society. Either he's trying to win approval and success or he's being mildly rebellious. But there's nothing in the gay's body or nervous system that makes his taste necessarily different; it's different because that's how he adapts to his situation.

Today, as straight society gradually becomes more accepting of gays, gay taste is changing. Piss-elegance is on the way out. Camp art has become almost as popular with straights as with gays, and is losing its appeal to many younger gays. Many liberated gays dress well but not in a gaudy or daring way, and many straight men now wear the kind of flowing shirts, snug slacks, and jewelry that only gays used to wear. The gap between gay taste and straight taste is not as great as it used to be.

And some day, when gays are fully accepted and the gay world and the straight world are no longer at war, there won't be any difference between gay taste and straight taste, because there won't be any need for gay taste to be different.

7

"QUEER" GAYS

"Fancy fruits"

On Christopher Street in New York's Greenwich Village, a grocery store has a sign reading FANCY FRUITS. Christopher Street is a well-known cruising ground for gay men in search of "instant sex," and it amuses some of them to gather under that sign, for "fruit," like "queer," is a mocking word for homosexual.

And queer they are in the eyes of straight passersby. Some wear flowered scarves, capes, and unbuttoned shirts, others are dressed in leather pants and metal-studded leather jackets, and still others wear blue jeans so tight that the shape of their sex organs shows plainly. They're all busy cruising: they idle along and study each other intently, and some make girlish, seductive eyes at each other and camp wildly, while others act "heavy" and tough; some hold hands, some walk with their arms around each other, and some couples press close together in doorways.

It's all very strange and disturbing to the straights who pass by and stare, frozen-faced and baffled. A gay man who lives on Christopher Street writes: "The tourists crowd by the thousands to watch us lead our exotic lives. The tourists are always watching through their sunglasses, watching whatever it is they imagine our lives to be." But who can blame them for watching, and for trying to figure out what these men think and feel and how they live? For the cruising gays on Christopher Street are the part of the homosexual world that is farthest from the straight world, the part that straights think of as "queer," not just in the sense of homosexual, but in the sense of peculiar, weird, or unnatural.

As we have already seen, there are many different kinds of homosexuals, and most of them don't look or act queer in this sense. In public they dress, speak, and behave much like straight people, and even in private some of them fall in love, care about each other, and make a home together in much the same way most straight people do. (We might even call them "straight" gays—but that's another matter, and we'll get to it in the next chapter.)

But there are many gays whose appearance and behavior, either after working hours or all the time, make them seem to straights as strange as creatures from another planet. Among gay men, the most obvious queer ones include the lisping nellie, the super-swishy "screaming queen," and the "drag queen" (a man wearing a woman's clothing and make-up). Many straights find these queer gays not only peculiar or "sick" but troubling, repulsive, and even infuriating. Even the liberals who favor equal rights for homosexuals are often made uncomfortable by the looks and behavior of the more extreme queer gays.

There are queer lesbians, too, though queerness is far less common among them. The great majority of lesbians do not look or act noticeably different in public from straight women, and even experienced lesbians can't usually spot others of their kind.[131] But a small number of lesbians do seem very noticeable and very peculiar to straights. The bull dyke is the most obvious kind; her mannish hair style, clothes, voice, and mannerisms call attention to themselves, and bother many straights. So do the looks and behavior of the radical lesbians, deliberately plain in dress, angry in manner, and loud and even violent in their public discussions and political demonstrations.

But why should straight people be upset, annoyed, or angered by the mere look of queer gays, as long as the gays lead their sex lives in private and only with other gays? What difference does it make how they dress, speak, or behave as long as they do no harm to straights?

Probably the main reason is that the most noticeable of the queer gays are the ones who look and act like people of the opposite sex. Each of us, as he or she grows up, learns a whole set of rules of speech, behavior, and right and wrong. That's a major part of what social scientists call the "culture" of our society. We feel annoyed and resentful when anyone breaks the rules of our culture, because we learn them so early and so thoroughly that they seem to us the proper or natural order of things. That's why a person who laughs at something sad seems evil—or crazy—to us; that's why a cowardly soldier or an unloving mother fills us with disgust and anger.

And so it is with sex roles. From babyhood on, we learn a thousand things about how girls and women are supposed to look, sound, and act, and a thousand similar things about boys and men. These days, even though many of the old rules have been discarded, we still expect a woman to dress, speak, walk, and act in a recognizably feminine fashion and a man in a recognizably masculine one. Our feeling of "right" and "wrong" about these things has been drilled into us so strongly that it bothers us, deep down, to see a man acting like a woman or a woman acting like a man—a switching around that social scientists call "role reversal." The nellie, although he is a man, plays the reverse role, that of a woman; the bull dyke, although she is a woman, plays the role of a man. And that's as upsetting to most straight people as it would be to a child if his father, one evening, started whining and fussing like a five-year-old, and asking the child for a cookie and a bedtime story.

Of course, role reversal is only part of the story. Many queer gays don't reverse their roles but exaggerate the ones that go with their own sex. On the various "Muscle Beaches" of California many of the most powerful and masculine-looking men are homosexuals, and so are the virile, dangerous-looking men, gotten up as motorcycle toughs, who get together in the gay "leather bars." Similarly, not all lesbians are bull dykes; many, in fact, are femmes with exaggerated feminine traits—heavy make-up, long eyelashes, tapering false fingernails, a coy and seductive manner, and girlish or ultra-feminine clothing.

But the Muscle Beach jocks and the femmes don't usually upset straights, because they seem to be doing the "natural" thing. The nellies aren't any more homosexual than the Muscle Beach jocks, and the bull dykes aren't any more homosexual than the femmes, but they seem queerer to straights because they're playing the "wrong" roles. Yet, in a sense, they *are* queerer than the jocks and the femmes, because they're waving the flag of rebellion at the straight world; they're "asking for trouble." And a person has to be rather peculiar to knowingly do something that is going to make trouble for himself or herself.

The pity of it is that there isn't any need for straights to be troubled by gay role reversal. In itself, it doesn't hurt anyone or anything. The aging "auntie" on the beach at Fire Island, strung with beads and flowers, and acting like a great lady to the handsome young men around him, isn't harming America any more than the weight lifter at Muscle Beach. The bull dyke with crewcut hair and a cigar, talking of "broads" and of "balling," isn't tearing down democracy any more than the pretty femme.

It's hard for straights to see this, because their reactions come from their unconscious feelings. It takes a lot of rethinking to overcome such feelings. But perhaps role reversal will go out of fashion before straights get used to it. Many young gays today think it's out of date for homosexuals to imitate the heterosexual world by taking either a masculine or a feminine role and playing either the nellie or the jock part, the femme or the butch part. Just what roles gays will play in the future isn't clear; maybe they'll find ways to behave that lie between the poles, blending various masculine and feminine traits in one person. They may still look a bit queer to straights, but not very—especially since straight men and women are becoming freer to borrow from each other than they used to be.

The gay view of queer gays

Some homosexuals may object angrily to our speaking of "queer" gays. They may call it a put-down, an expression of scorn and contempt. So let's agree that we—the author of this book and its readers—aren't being scornful or contemptuous when we use this term; we're only being descriptive. The behavior and, often, the looks of the kinds of gays we're talking about are very odd, very unlike what we usually expect of other people; that's what we mean by calling them queer gays.

Indeed, some homosexuals themselves speak of certain kinds of gays as "queer queers." And it was homosexuals who invented, and who regularly use, slang terms of amusement and ridicule for the various kinds of queer gays. It is homosexuals, more often than straights, who call effeminate, show-off male gays "nellie queens," "screaming queens," and "flaming faggots," and who call men who dress as women "drag queens." It is gays themselves who speak sneeringly of the "bitchiness" of many of the queer gays, and who call femmes "floozies" and make fun of the bull dyke for "thinking she's got balls."

Some gays even refer to the particularly queer ones as "deviants," "freaks," and "trash."[132]

But it isn't just straight gays who talk like this; queer gays do it, too. For although militant gays say they're proud to be gay, most others aren't; they look down on gayness somewhat, and therefore make fun of it. Even though most gays learn to accept their own homosexuality, many of them continue to have some bad feelings about it. More than one out of every four male gays, for instance, feels he hasn't enough respect for himself, and over half of male gays admit that knowing themselves to be homosexual makes them feel somewhat (or even very) guilty, depressed, anxious, or ashamed.[133] And those who feel this way about homosexuality in themselves are bound to feel the same way about it in others. To the extent that they think ill of themselves, they think ill of those who are like them. As one supposedly proud gay liberationist has written:[134]

> Homosexuals develop a great sense of guilt about themselves; for myself, however much I try, I doubt if I shall ever totally lose that. Guilt, in turn, produces self-hatred, and those who hate themselves will find it difficult not to despise others who share their guilt.

Now, of course, this is not true of all homosexuals. But it *is* true of many of the queer ones—and the queerer they are, the more cruelly they make fun of other queer gays and the more contemptuous they are of the out-and-out freaks. That's why the conversation and writing of so many gays is filled with self-mockery, and with jokes and wisecracks that they would be furious to hear coming from straights. Just imagine how they'd feel if straights had named a gay magazine *Fag Rag*, a gay radio show "Fruit Punch," or a gay drama group "Purple Pansy Productions." But straights didn't; gays did, in each case.

Thus, the self-dislike of many of the queer gays is the reason for much of their nastiness and bitchiness to each other, their name calling, their fighting, their unfaithfulness. And worse. One young man who used to go "tricking" in the park (having instant sex with strangers) discovered that he had an active case of syphilis. Instead of going to a doctor, for months he stepped up his sexual activity. Later, he admitted to a psychologist why: he was trying to give the disease to as many other gay men as he could before starting medical treatment.

That isn't typical of gay behavior—but it's an extreme example of how the queerer kind of gays feel about other gays.

Deviants

Gays, as we've seen, are particularly scornful of those extreme types they themselves sometimes call deviants or trash. The several kinds of persons classified as deviants make up only a small part of the gay population, but they get most of the headlines and the bad publicity. It is they, more than all other gays combined, who keep alive in the minds of straight people most of the ugly myths and beliefs about homosexuals. That's why most gays, even if they are tolerant of deviants, avoid social contact with them, and why some gays strongly dislike and resent them. As one gay man said to a sociologist, "It's too bad that so much of the world judges all gay people by a few of the social deviants that throw a bad light on all of us."

Here are the main kinds of deviants.

Drag queens and transvestites: These are people who "cross-dress"—that is, who dress in the clothing of the other sex. Cross-dressing occurs in both directions, but it's much more common for men to dress as women than the other way around.

All cross-dressing seems queer to most straights, but gays see some of it as less freaky, some of it as more freaky. The less freaky kind is known as "drag." A gay man who dresses and makes up as a woman and appears in public in a spirit of camp or play-acting, making no effort to fool anyone, is known to gays as a drag queen. He's a giant step beyond the nellie or screaming queen in queerness, but some gays regard what he's doing as fun, satire, and even artistry. In some large cities, gays hold elegant drag shows, drag balls, and drag beauty-contests; the audience gets a special kick out of the fact that the beautiful "women" on stage or on the dance floor are actually gay men, and no one, including the drag queens, pretends that they're anything but that.

But many other gays—especially the straight ones—consider drag queens to be freaks and show-offs. And they're particularly embarrassed or disgusted by the ones in "radical drag"—the queens who wear mustaches or full beards along with their make-up, wigs, and female clothing, in order to look particularly ridiculous and shocking.

The "real" or "true" transvestite is nothing like the

drag queen. When gays or sex researchers speak of a true transvestite, they mean a man or woman who not only dresses as the opposite sex but seriously believes, and wants others to believe, that he or she actually *is* some-one of the other sex. (Again, this is much more common among men than among women.)

Some transvestites dress up only in private. A man who may not ever perform homosexual acts will secretly put on women's clothes and, in a daydream, think of himself as a woman for a few hours. Even the closest friends of such a transvestite may never know his secret. Psychologists and straights consider such behavior a definite emotional illness—and so do most gays. It certainly sounds that way: one such transvestite man, for instance, speaks of "the woman within," and tells of "the exquisite joy of being able to be Dorothy for the evening, manicuring and painting my nails and feeling that everything I'm wearing is just right."

Other male transvestites play their part in public and make every effort to have other people accept them as women. They give themselves female names, speak of themselves as women, and insist on being treated as women. They are often very flirtatious with men, especially butch gay men. Some are prostitutes of a special sort, serving those borderline gay men who want to pretend that their sex partners aren't other males. Here's how one transvestite prostitute, who calls himself Marcia, talks about it:[135]

> I don't like straight men. There's only one thing they want—to get up your dress. They're really insulting to

women. [But] there's a lot of gay men that prefer transvestites. It's mostly bisexual type men, you know, they
like to go both ways but don't like anybody to know what's
happening. Rather than pick up a gay man, they'll pick up
a gay transvestite. Lots of times they tell me, "You're not
a woman!" I say, "I don't know what I am if I'm not a
woman." I say, "Honey, let me tell you something, you
can either take it or leave it." If they take me, they got to
take me as I want them to take me.

It's not easy to understand how or why anyone would
think this way. Sex researchers have several theories about
it, but probably the best-accepted one is that the real
transvestite is a homosexual man who hates being homosexual. He can accept his desire for sex with other men
only by making believe that he is a woman; if he can
fool himself into thinking so, then he feels that having
sex with other men is all right.[136] Such thinking is much
like that of insane people. And indeed, nearly all gays,
including most of the queer ones, recognize it as somewhat crazy and think of true transvestites as "sickies" and
deviants.

Transsexuals: These people—usually men—go beyond
transvestism in their desire to be of the other sex. Transvestism isn't good enough because, whenever the transvestite gets undressed, he is confronted by the truth. According to Dr. John Money, the medical psychologist, the
transsexual depises his male sex organs and wants to get
rid of them and of his male appearance.[137] So he takes
female hormones in pill form to make his breasts swell,
he has his facial hair removed by electrolysis, and he has a

surgeon remove his sex organs and create a vagina out of his own skin.

By now, thousands of men have undergone such treatment and become women, more or less. A number of them have even married, and some say they have satisfactory sex with their husbands. (Women, too, can have transsexual operations and treatment, but few have done so because surgeons cannot yet create a penis that actually works like a real one.) Usually, these transsexuals deny that they were ever homosexuals or ever had homosexual desires; they claim that they were females trapped in male bodies, and had a female's desires. But most sex researchers say that transsexualism is an extreme form of homosexuality, and that most transsexuals could not bear the thought that they were homosexual and therefore convinced themselves that they were really women who only needed surgery to correct nature's mistake.[138]

The gay community is predominantly unsympathetic to transsexuals and regards them as freaks because they mutilate their bodies rather than admit their own homosexuality.

Leather freaks: Homosexual men who dress in leather clothing, and look and act like tough cycle bums or cowboys, are known among gays as "leather freaks." They seek to appear super-butch, dominant, and cruel, because homosexuality of that kind is acceptable to them; the one thing they can't stand is to be thought effeminate or tender.

Their cruelty isn't only a matter of looks; in *The Gay Mystique*, Peter Fisher estimates that more than half the leather freaks practice S/M. S/M, as we saw earlier, stands for sadomasochism—the giving and receiving of pain as part of the sexual act. In sadomasochistic sex, one partner is the sadist ("master," in S/M slang), and the other is the masochist ("slave"). The master gets a special sexual thrill out of tying up the slave, beating or whipping him, and then more or less raping him—and the slave gets a special sexual thrill out of being treated this way.

Leather freaks are a small but noticeable part of the gay world—and most gays wish they weren't; Peter Fisher says that they're an even greater embarrassment to the gay world than transvestites. Gays sometimes kid each other about using whips and chains, but in actual fact most of them consider serious S/M bizarre and deviant.[139]

Hustlers and johns: The hustler, you remember, is a young male—a teen-ager or a young adult—who takes money from an older male, or a "john," to let the john fellate him. Many hustlers think of themselves as straight; they claim that they're just earning money and that the john, fellating them because he *wants* to, is the real queer.

But the gay world considers both the hustler and the john to be outside the limits of "normal" homosexual behavior. The john is often a married closet gay who secretly looks for a male prostitute from time to time and pays for a "quickie." Gays find this queer, just as straights do. As for the hustler, most gays look down on him for maintaining that he's really straight; even when a hustler admits his own homosexuality, most gays consider him trash for selling himself, and feel that associating with him would harm their reputation.[140]

Chickenhawks: These are men who seek out young

boys ("chicken") for homosexual acts. Sometimes the chicken is a runaway boy or teen-ager who performs sex acts for a living, like a hustler. Hustlers are a bit older and work for themselves; chickens usually have "pimps" (managers) who protect them, find johns for them, and take most of their earnings. Sometimes, however, the chicken is an innocent young boy or teen-ager whom the chicken-hawk tries to seduce. Whichever kind the chickenhawk is interested in, most gays feel only contempt for him. In the first place, he is often a married closet gay, and therefore, as gays see it, "not one of us." In the second place, gays resent the chickenhawk because, like transvestites and transsexuals, he gives the straight world a distorted notion of homosexuality. In the third place, most gays are as opposed to child molesting, on humane grounds, as most straights are.[141]

Cruising

Cruising, or tricking, among gays, involves going to certain kinds of public places in search of "instant sex" with a stranger. Gay cruisers exchange a few words, or perhaps nothing but a meaningful look. Then, if both are willing, they immediately go off and have sex in the nearest convenient place—a men's room, an alleyway, a clump of bushes, the nearby apartment of one of them. As soon as they have finished, they usually go their separate ways and never meet again. At most, they may make a one-night stand of it and part in the morning without telling each other their real names and with no intention of ever getting together again.

There is a certain amount of cruising in the straight world, but it hardly compares with that in the gay world. The majority of straight people are married and most of these don't cruise. As for unmarried straights, most either never cruise or do so only for brief periods of time, while looking for a steady relationship. When they do cruise, they rarely proceed to sex as swiftly and with as little personal relationship as gays do.

But among male gays, cruising is widespread, and for many of them it is a way of life. Two thirds of the gay men in the recent survey made by the Kinsey Institute said that they cruise regularly; four out of ten do so at least once a week, and some do so every day.[142] Lesbians, on the other hand, behave much more like straights: four out of five gay women hadn't cruised at all in the past year, and those who had did their cruising at parties rather than in public places.[143] Usually, too, cruising lesbians spend a fair amount of time getting to know each other before having sex.

To those straights who know about gay cruising, it seems one of the queerest sides of gay life. What makes it seem so is that it is almost totally impersonal. Most of the time, each partner knows nothing about the other except what he looks like—and doesn't want to know any more. What counts is physical appeal and the willingness to perform certain sexual acts—but neither partner wants to know what the other is like as a human being or to have any personal contact either before or after the sex act. Both partners understand this; it is the basic rule of the cruising game. Some animals mate and part in the same way, but among straight human beings there is almost nothing like it except prostitution. Most gay cruising, however, isn't prostitution; it's the way in which many gays prefer to have sex—completely cut off from the rest of their feelings and their lives.

Gay cruising takes place in a number of different kinds of places. Here are the major ones:

Gay bars: These are the downtown of gay life—the center of gay socializing and recreation. In recent years, as police pressure has eased up in many large cities, gay bars have multiplied; one estimate says there are now four thousand throughout the country.[144] Many gay bars attract special kinds of customers: there are lesbian bars, nellie bars, butch bars, leather bars, and so on. The gay bar is a refuge, a shelter from the straight world, a place where gays can stop pretending and can be themselves. As one lesbian says, the bar is like a sorority, a club, or even a home.

But a curious home. There is some chatter going on, and sometimes even dancing, but the social life is only an excuse for being here; the real purpose is to cruise—and therefore the mood in most gay bars is not warm and friendly but tense, competitive, and even hostile.[145] Straights who wander into a gay bar by mistake often can't figure out what's going on: the patrons stand about, many alone, silently staring at each newcomer, or engaging in brittle, nervous conversations while studying other people and making eyes at them—or avoiding their glances. Many gays who cruise the bars hate it; one of them speaks bitterly of "the hard looks, the coldness, the self-protective shell" of the typical bar cruisers—but probably he himself seems that way to the others.

There also is a certain amount of cruising by gays in

what appear to be straight male bars. Men in such bars who look thoroughly butch and claim to be absolutely straight may be on the lookout for a passive gay man, and some passive gays go to these bars to be sought out. One such gay describes the situation:

> In a gay bar I'm hardly even noticed, but in a redneck bar one out of every four or five guys I talk to ends up chasing me. Truck-drivers, laborers, deliverymen, all completely straight (ho-ho!). A few drinks, and they're telling me how they hate gays. Then the bar closes and they want to come to my place for a nightcap. It always ends up the same way—they're the active ones, very aggressive, insist on penetrating. And then maintain, as they leave, that they're really straight.

Gay baths: In nearly every major city there are health clubs for gay men, but the real business in the clubs is cruising. Cruising in the baths is even more impersonal and nonsocial than in the bars: there is practically no conversation, and sex acts take place right on the premises, often in front of onlookers.

Gay baths have lockers, steam rooms, showers, a pool, exercise rooms, and sometimes bars and snack rooms. The patrons sometimes swim, steam themselves, or exercise, but most of the time they are busy cruising. In the steam rooms and lounges, a number of men will sit around naked, looking at each other; some of them fellate others while the rest watch. Elsewhere in the club there are rows of small rooms for rent, and men walk up and down the halls outside these rooms waiting for invitations to come in. An invitation may consist of a few words ("What's your hurry?"), or simply a nod or smile. Or even less: if the door is left open, that means the person inside is willing to have sex with anyone who enters. Often, not a word is spoken: the visitor comes in, has sex with the man in the room, and then leaves. It is quite common for a customer at the baths to have sex with several strangers during one evening, and men who stay in a room with the door open and who play the passive (insertee) part sometimes have a dozen or more partners in a night.[146]

As peculiar or even "sick" as this may seem to most straight people, it seems perfectly reasonable to a good many gays. The baths are second in popularity only to bars as places to cruise (some cities have a dozen or more of them), and there are so many in the United States that the owners and managers of gay baths recently held a week-long convention, like other businessmen, to discuss their business problems and methods of dealing with them.

Restrooms: Some gay men go to certain public toilets, known in their slang as "tearooms," to have sex with strangers. After making eye contact (usually, no word is spoken), two of them will go into a stall and one will perform fellatio on the other. The active partner (insertor) usually leaves immediately afterward, but the passive partner sometimes stays and services other visitors, one after another, for hours.[147]

Many gays rate those who are involved in "tearoom trade" as "queer queers," because the whole thing is so ugly and because many tearoom visitors are married closet queens. But some members of the gay community insist that they like tearoom sex just because it is so impersonal, so free of emotional ties. As one of them writes: "I like making it in a restroom. There's romance in the fear of being caught, the excitement of making it with a complete stranger. No piss-elegant romantic trappings, no bed, just cold tile floor and cold ceramic toilet bowl, no pretensions [or] future commitments."[148]

Other cruising grounds: Not all cruising is as impersonal as that in the baths and tearooms. Lesbians and some gay men cruise chiefly at parties and dances, and many gay men cruise on beaches, in city parks, and on the street, where they pretend to be window-shopping. In most of these situations, the cruising is likely to involve conversation and socializing before sex.

But some cruising grounds involve even less personal communication than the baths and the tearooms. In New York, for instance, there is a waterfront area where empty trucks and vans, parked overnight, are used by cruising gays. They wander around the trucks at night, and when they hear sexual activity going on in one of them, they climb in and take "pot luck" in the dark with people they not only never speak to but never even see.

The strangest thing about this is that many of the gays who cruise in such places do so not because they have no other choice but because they like it. As one young artist —a gentle and sensitive man—says: "I love cruising in the park, and even in the trucks. Strangers in the night, you know—it's so exciting! You never know what you'll find, or what kind of person you'll connect with. And the chance that you might get busted or beaten up lends a terrific zing. It's crazy of me, but I just *adore* it!"

The loners

The thing straights notice least about queer gays is the most painful fact about their lives: its terrible loneliness. For most queer gays are bachelors and live alone, most are cut off from close contact with the straight world, and, above all, most cruise rather than enter into warm, steady relationships with other gays.

Cruising is a lonely business; even in a crowded bar, each man is in competition with the others, each is on his own and out for himself. And it is a lonely business in a deeper sense: a person who is promiscuous—who has quickie sex with many strangers—never makes human contact with his partners, even when their bodies are connected. For a few moments, he may have a sense of "with-ness"—but then the act is finished, the partner hurries away, and the illusion vanishes like a bursting bubble.

Yet a gay who is lonely may cruise desperately and continually, because he gets temporary relief from each trick. The playwright Tennessee Williams, recalling a time of intense cruising in his own life, says, "It was a period of loneliness. Promiscuity was better than nothing." And another gay says that in one lonely two-year span he had 150 different sex partners—"but that sustained me, kept me sane."

The combination of promiscuity and loneliness is quite

common among gays. The Kinsey researchers, in their new survey, show that most gay men suffer from loneliness anywhere from occasionally to very often, and that most gay men are definitely promiscuous, at least for some years.[149] The average gay man has one thousand different sex partners in a lifetime, most of whom are strangers and one-time partners. In contrast, the average straight man has from five to nine sex partners in a lifetime, most of them persons he cares about and has sex with repeatedly.[150] Lesbians are far less promiscuous than gay men; they are much more like straight women in this respect, though they tend to have somewhat more sex partners in the course of a lifetime than straight women do.[151]

Gays who cruise can name many reasons why quickie gay sex is better than affection-laden heterosexual sex. They say things like, "You don't have to play any games or strike any poses. You just sidle up and pop the question." Or, "It's more direct and honest than heterosexual situations. You don't have to pretend love." A militant lesbian says she felt truly "free" when she first managed to go to bed with a strange woman, have a good time, and then say goodbye, without any burden of emotion or romance. And a gay man, speaking as many cruisers do, says, "Now is now and let's enjoy it. Tomorrow is another day."

But these brave words are like the boasts of the grasshopper; when the winter of loneliness comes, he's a pathetic thing. Gay promiscuity, whatever its pleasures, comes at a high cost. Not VD, though that's often part of it; not arrest, muggings, or beatings, though they're part of it, too. But they're the lesser part; the greater part of the cost is loneliness. Quickie sex may seem to relieve loneliness, but ends by making it worse; like alcohol or drugs, it kills the pain briefly and then leaves the addict in worse shape than ever. As the editors of *Gay* magazine recently told their readers: "Quickie sex often seems to suffice for months at a time. [But] what starts early in one's experience as a way of avoiding involvement can become a lifestyle that leaves in its wake a genuine emptiness."

The key words in that comment are "a way of avoiding involvement." Many queer gays are lonely because they're afraid to have a real involvement or don't like themselves well enough to like and trust other gays.[152] Instead, they have sex only with strangers, and never take a chance on loving anyone. In the recent Kinsey survey, the gays who suffered most from loneliness were the very ones who had the poorest opinion of themselves, had the most emotional and psychological problems, and had no intimate relationships. And this is a very common situation: most gay men have never had an exclusive relationship with another gay that lasted half a year or more, and three out of ten gay men have never had *any* relationship longer than a one-night stand.[153]

Lesbians are a different story. The great majority of them have had one to a few close relationships that lasted a good while. Nearly all lesbians believe they want a lifelong or at least long-term love relationship, but they seem to have trouble staying in love more than a few years. They don't cruise, though; they keep falling in love again.[154]

The really queer thing about gay men who cruise is that they so sharply separate sex from affectionate feelings. It's as if they consider sex dirty and love clean. They even stay away from sex with their gay friends. As one man explained it to a researcher: "I think if you have sex with a friend it will destroy the friendship. I think that in the inner mind we all respect high moral standards, and none of us want to feel low in the eyes of anybody else."[155] Sex and affection, he was saying, don't go together; in fact, one spoils the other. And that, in the view of most straight people, is about as queer a way to look at things as there can be.

8

"STRAIGHT"

GAYS

For lack of a better name—

"Straight" gays?

Sounds ridiculous, doesn't it? All along, we've been saying that straight is the opposite of gay, that straight means heterosexual and gay means homosexual.

But a small number of gay men and a large number of lesbians are more like the straight people all around them than they are like the queer gays described in the last chapter. Almost no one in the heterosexual world even knew such gays existed until recently. It was only some twenty years ago that a few of them asked Dr. Evelyn Hooker to start making a scientific study of "their kind" of homosexual—the unknown kind who are psychologically healthy and who lead relatively stable, occupationally successful lives.

Since that time—and especially in the last few years—

social scientists have learned a good deal about gays of this sort.[156] In many important ways, they resemble heterosexuals—that is, healthy and successful heterosexuals. For one thing, their lives aren't split into separate parts, walled off from each other; they're not closet queens, living as married straights and sneaking off once a week or so for an evening's orgy at the baths. For another thing, they're content to look, dress, and act in ways that are usual and acceptable in straight society; they're not screaming queens, leather freaks, bull dykes, or drag queens. For a third, they have long-lasting love relationships, much as most heterosexuals do; they're not loners, bar cruisers, tearoom trade, hustlers, or patrons of the baths.

They get up and go to work, have dinner at home most of the time, live with the person they love, visit friends, clean the house, pay their bills, rewire lamps, and have Christmas dinner with their parents. Some of them are business people, some are waiters, there are some in almost every occupation you can think of. Some watch TV while others go to the theater. Some like Big Macs while others eat only fine gourmet food. Some read popular magazines while others read the latest and most intellectual books. Some vote Republican and some Democratic. In short, in most ways they're a cross-section of America, and in most ways resemble straights more than they do queer gays.

So we do need a name for them. One gay writer calls them "normal" homosexuals, but this implies that all other gays are abnormal, and as we've seen, that's far from true. In California, many gays call them "elite" homosexuals, but that has a snobbish sound to it; besides, elite means upper-class or influential, and some of the un-queer gays are working-class and without much social influence. Still other people prefer to call them "healthy" homosexuals, but this makes it sound as if all other gays are sick, which is a great exaggeration.

That's why the expression "straight gays" may be a good one after all, because it says that these people are homo-sexual, but that in most ways they belong to and fit into the straight world they live in.

The social life of straight gays

The social life of straight gays is very different from that of queer gays. Queer gays, as we've seen, tend to spend their leisure time in public places such as gay bars, baths, and other sexual "marketplaces," as Dr. Hooker calls them. In any such marketplace, the relationships between people are bound to be both shallow and fiercely competi-tive. Friendship is brittle and often more like enmity; the "crowd" is not held together by any strong ties but is always changing, especially because many queer gays are young drifters who work a little and then quit for a while, and frequently move from one rented room or dingy pad to another.

Straight gays, in contrast, are usually somewhat older (in their thirties and up), have careers or steady jobs, and live in apartments or houses that they make into real homes. Most important, the majority of them live in pairs—couples, united by sex and affection—much like married heterosexuals. For these reasons, their social life is much like that of heterosexual married people: they meet in each other's homes for drinks, cocktail parties, dinner parties, and evenings of conversation or bridge. Except in a very few parts of the country, however, they're not likely to belong to social clubs, community organizations, or other groups made up of married couples; they'd probably be rejected, or even if accepted, they wouldn't "fit in."

When straight gays socialize, their talk and their behavior isn't exactly like that of heterosexuals. Often there is a special gay flavor to the subjects that straight gays talk about, or a touch of campiness in some of their words or actions. But a heterosexual in their midst might not realize, for a while, what sort of group he was in; indeed, gays refer to a heterosexual who does know (and is not critical of them) as being "wise."

It used to be most unusual for straight gays to socialize with heterosexuals, even wise ones. Sometimes straight gays worked alongside heterosexuals who knew, and sometimes they had one or two old friends who understood and were sympathetic. But, by and large, most socializing between gays and heterosexuals was forced and largely false—and therefore rare. The gays pretended to be heterosexual, and the heterosexuals, even if they suspected the truth, pretended that they didn't. Each side was afraid to be honest. The gays were afraid that if they ever were truthful and open about themselves, the heterosexuals would turn against them. The heterosexuals were afraid that if the subject ever came out in the open, they wouldn't know how to act or what to say; some of them, too, probably feared that if they admitted they knew about the gays, the gays might feel free to make sexual approaches to them.

That's how things used to be—and still are in many parts of America. But the new liberalism of young heterosexuals and the new openness of some gays are making changes. In certain social circles, especially in the more liberal parts of the country, straight gays and wise heterosexuals are beginning to mix socially, and to invite each other to their homes for dinner and other social get-togethers. More and more straight gays are beginning to be honest and open with those heterosexuals they value as friends, because only when both sides are honest can they be genuinely close to each other and truly comfortable in their socializing. This is how one gay man, the thirty-year-old vice-president of a small insurance brokerage in New York, explains it:[157]

I had a great many straight friends and I had to come to the point of deciding if I wanted to be split from these friends, or try to keep them on the side, or to involve them in my life. And I finally made a decision that if I wanted to keep them as friends, they would have to know about me. I would have to be able to share things with them. So I told all of my straight friends about my situation, and there have been varied reactions, but generally all of the people whom I considered good friends before I told them, really close friends, are probably even closer now.

A lesbian couple in Dallas had become friendly with a married heterosexual couple they knew in business. Even though they often met socially, and it was clear that the lesbians lived together, the nature of the relationship of the two women was never mentioned. But one night after the two couples had had a marvelous dinner, they started talking about a movie that touched on homosexuality and suddenly, somehow, the lesbians began to tell their friends about themselves. "We're gay. We're not just business partners, we're 'married.' We want you to know." The husband and wife looked pleased, and said they were glad the two had told them.

"We *had* to," said one of the lesbians, "because we love you and want to be able to share things with you. It's such a relief to have you know."

"To have us know?" said the husband. "But of course we *knew*. We sensed it long ago, when we began to spend some time with you."

"Yes," said the lesbian, "and we sort of knew that you knew. But now we've said it to you and there's no more need to pretend. And that makes all the difference. You can't know how good it feels to us."

"Maybe we can," said the man's wife, "because it feels very good to *us* that you trusted us enough to tell us."

Gay love

The biggest difference between queer gays and straight gays has to do with love. When people speak of "homosexual love" or "gay love," they usually mean homosexual sex acts rather than the emotional relationship we call love. We often refer to sexual activity as "making love," but people can make love without loving each other—and can love each other even if, for one reason or another, they don't make love. The question is, can gays do more than make love? Can they love each other?

The love of two adults for each other has long seemed, to people in our civilization, to be one of the most important and desirable things in life. Nearly all that has been said and written about it has to do with the love of a man and a woman for each other—especially the love that blossoms before marriage but grows and deepens after the two become husband and wife. This kind of love is a blend of many things: it is partly romance but partly everyday practicality; it is giving but also getting; it is trusting but also being trusted; it is taking care of the other but also being taken care of. It has anger and fighting in it, but also making up and being closer than ever. It is partly physical desire and sex, but even more the sharing of experiences, of hopes, of fears, of pleasures, of sorrows. Above all, it gives each partner the feeling of *belonging*, and a sense of *completeness*, as if the other partner were the missing half of the self.

That's the kind of love most young men and women hope to find with someone of the opposite sex; most of them do find it, to some degree, and build their marriages upon it. But what about homosexuals? Can they feel anything like this for each other? Most heterosexuals find it hard to imagine how gays could do so. And certainly there doesn't seem to be anything remotely like this sort of love in the homosexual relationships that exist among the more obvious queer gays, most of whom don't seem interested in—or even able to have—such feelings.

But straight gays have feelings and needs of a very different sort from those of the queer gays. Many straight gays are capable of homosexual love that is as complex, as deep, and as important to them as the love of a man and a woman for each other. Naturally, homosexual love is different from heterosexual love in a number of ways, but in an even larger number of ways it's very much like it.

Here are some of the ways in which gay love resembles —and differs from—heterosexual love.

The purposes of marriage: Gays who love each other and live together often say that they are "married," and many hundreds of such couples have even gone through wedding ceremonies to show each other and their friends how they feel about one another. But gay "marriage" differs from heterosexual marriage in several important respects.

No state recognizes such marriages as legal, and therefore gay couples can't file joint tax returns, aren't entitled to social security widowhood benefits if one of them dies, can't get married persons' insurance rates, and so on.[158] A few gay activists are fighting the present laws in court, hoping that judges will decide that same-sex couples have the same right to be legally married as heterosexual couples.

And in a real sense, gay marriage does have most of the same purposes as heterosexual marriage. The great exception, of course, is parenthood: obviously, gays don't pair up in order to have children. But even among heterosexuals, having and raising children is no longer the chief purpose of marriage these days. If it were, couples who have children would stay together for their children's sake—yet if love dies, most of them get divorced. For nowadays the main purpose of heterosexual marriage is to satisfy certain emotional needs, among them the need for intimacy, familiarity, belonging, security, trust, companionship, and love. And according to Dr. Ralph Blair, editor of the *Homosexual Counseling Journal*, gay marriage satisfies these needs for gay people just as heterosexual marriage does for heterosexual people.

That's why a gay man or a lesbian can feel as excited, when meeting someone of the same sex who seems "right," as a man and a woman can about each other. That's why gays can be as romantic in their courting as heterosexuals. That's why in a gay love affair, as in a heterosexual one, the lovers can start with feelings of romantic infatuation, proceed to fall in love, come to care about each other very deeply, and finally decide that they want to live together as a couple.

Chances of finding love: Today nearly all heterosexuals have one or more love affairs before they marry, and over nine tenths of all heterosexuals eventually marry, most of them before they're thirty. Gay men, in contrast, aren't very good at finding love or falling in love. Many of them have passing crushes on other gays—infatuations that last for a few days or weeks—but fewer than half of them (according to one recent survey) have ever had a love relationship that lasted as long as six months.[159] At the time of the survey only about one fifth of the men were having a long-term love relationship. Some sociologists think the reason gay males have so little success in finding love or keeping it is the disapproval of straight society, which makes them dislike themselves—and dislike anyone who is like themselves. Others think the problem is that most male gays are immature or neurotic or are so quick to have sex that they never take time to learn to care about each other.

Whatever the reason or reasons, things are changing: a small but growing number of gay men want to find deep, loving relationships.[160] One out of every six gay men in a recent survey said that finding a single long-term or permanent relationship was "the most important thing in life."[161] And as the social pressure against gays eases up, more of them are finding it possible to do so.

Unlike gay men, nearly all lesbians want a deep, long-lasting love. Over two thirds of them have already had—or are having—such a relationship by the time they're in their twenties, and throughout their adult lives most lesbians are either in a love relationship or looking for the next one. Very few of them are loners, and very few cruise, except when they're between love affairs.[162]

The lifespan of love: Nearly two thirds of all heterosexual marriages last for a lifetime, and even those that break up last six or seven years, on the average. Gay marriage is much more fragile and breaks down far sooner; most marriages of gay men and of lesbians break up within about three years.[163] Of course, that's only the majority of them; a minority do last longer—ten years, twenty years, and occasionally a lifetime.

Sex researchers have offered many reasons why gay love is so often short-lived. One is that gay lovers, hiding themselves away from the outside world, are too close for their own good and too dependent on each other. Another is that often they are too much alike; they don't complete each other so much as mirror each other—and it's boring to be with one's own reflection all the time. One psychologist, after praising gay love to the skies, admits that, compared to heterosexual love, gay love is "over-close," "fatigue-prone," and "trigger-sensitive," and that even the tiniest whisper of disagreement can often cause violent conflict and lead to the breakup of the relationship.[164]

This isn't to say that gay love can't be as good as heterosexual love. It can; there are many examples to prove the point. But probably for a long while to come, gay love will be more fragile than heterosexual love because of the disapproval the lovers feel all around them, which forces them to be closer and more dependent on each other than is good for them. Yet it does seem that in a friendly environment, a gay love that is a good fit rather than a mirroring can be as deep, warm, tender, and idealistic as heterosexual love. And in terms of conversation, casual shows of affection, sex, the sharing of tasks, the working out of little disagreements, and the thousand little details of everyday life, such a gay marriage is almost indistinguishable from heterosexual marriage. As one gay man, himself a partner in a successful homosexual marriage, puts it, "Homosexuals can live the same kind of life their parents lived." But he might have added: "If they live in a community that accepts them."

Who is the "husband," who is the "wife"?: Most straight people assume that, in gay couples, one partner is the "husband," the masculine half, and the other the "wife," the feminine half, and that the masculine one does the jobs that husbands have traditionally done and the feminine one the jobs that wives have traditionally done.

But these days even heterosexuals don't divide things up as traditionally as they used to. Many wives work, and many husbands help with homemaking and child care. Some women repair household appliances and some men do much of the cooking. There is more "role sharing" today than ever—more taking turns at, or evenly dividing, the tasks that used to be performed exclusively by one marital partner or the other.

That's true of gay couples, too. In the past, many gay couples tried to imitate heterosexual marriage, with one being the money earner and the other the homemaker, one being butch and the other nellie or femme, one doing the heavy work and mechanical repairs and the other doing the homemaking and arranging of their social life. Even today, some gay couples still follow this pattern. But more often the partners in a gay marriage now share the major tasks; each, for instance, may do some of the housekeeping, and each may earn money. As for the other tasks, they split them up according to personal ability and preference: the nellie or the femme of the pair may be the chief fixer and repairer of mechanical things; the manly-looking male or the dykey lesbian may be the better cook and home decorator.

It isn't surprising, then, that these days heterosexuals often can't figure out which gay is the husband and which is the wife. Much of the time the question has no answer. Except, perhaps, the one given by a gay man to a sex researcher: "We're just a couple of happily married husbands," he said.

Identity: When a man and woman marry, they get a new identity in their society—they become a *pair*, a couple, husband-and-wife, the Smiths, Joneses, or whatever their name is. They're invited to social events not individually but as a couple. They're introduced to people as a couple. There's no vagueness, no uncertainty, about their identity.

Homosexual couples, however, have such an identity only among their closest friends; to the rest of the world they're still two separate persons. They don't even have a generally acceptable word by which to refer to each other, like the words "husband" and "wife" that heterosexuals have. Some gays refer to their partner as "my lover," but this conveys more the feeling of a temporary love affair than a long-term, marriage-like relationship. Some gays say "my friend," others "my companion," still others "my mate" or "my roommate," and so on; none is exactly right. Our language, one lesbian complains, "is bereft of a word to describe women who are sharing and building a life together," and the same is true for gay men.

But it isn't just a matter of a missing word. It's a matter of uncertain identity. If a gay man is invited to a company dinner, can he assume—as a married heterosexual would—that he should bring his mate? Does he dare? How would he introduce him? If a heterosexual acquaintance who doesn't know he has a mate—or who may not even be sure that he's gay—invites him to a party, what should he do? What will happen if he comes with his mate? What about visiting the folks at Christmas—should a gay take his mate along? And how should he introduce him to Dad and Mom? How should a gay introduce his or her mate to a heterosexual who isn't wise? It seems awkward to say, "I'd like you to meet my lover." But "I'd like you to meet John Doe" or "I'd like you to meet Jane Doe" is insulting, because it doesn't acknowledge that person's importance.

Some therapists and sociologists believe that the weakness of gay marriages—their tendency to break up early —is due to this lack of outside support. The world around the couple doesn't treat them as a definite team, doesn't respect their union. And each partner resents this—and often takes out his or her resentment on the guiltless cause of it all: the loved one.

Infidelity: Both heterosexual marriages and gay marriages can break up for many reasons—fighting, boredom, sexual problems, the struggle to be boss, among others. Including, of course, infidelity—having sex with someone outside the marriage.

But in heterosexual marriages infidelity is not nearly as common as it is in gay marriages. About half of all husbands and three quarters of all wives are faithful for as long as they are married.[165] But in the marriages of gay men, especially the younger ones, about three quarters of the partners start being unfaithful after a year—or even less—of living together.[166] Even among more mature gay men, many of the married are regularly unfaithful to each other. Lesbians, on the other hand, are much more likely to be faithful to each other at all ages, at least as long as they consider themselves in love and married.[167]

Most gays and sex researchers agree that infidelity is the most common reason that marriages between gay men break up. These "divorces" can cause just as much pain and suffering as heterosexual divorces. Why, then, don't gay men control the urge to have sex outside, in order to preserve their marriages? Apparently because the psychological need for variety and for new sexual conquest is unusually great among male gays, even among the straight ones. But in a few marriages of young gay men, and about half of the marriages of middle-aged gay men, the partners do remain faithful—either because they don't feel the need of new conquests, or because they love each other too much to risk hurting each other.

Many gays are scornful of those who think fidelity is important. Heterosexuals, they say, have always made a big fuss about fidelity because they wanted to be sure their children were their own. But for gays to insist on fidelity is to imitate heterosexuals, in order to win their approval. As one militant gay sees it, fidelity between gays is "the ultimate sellout to the straight establishment." So a number of married gays have been trying "open marriage" arrangements—bringing in outside visitors for a night of three-way or four-way sex, or going together to sex parties, or agreeing that each partner is free to go out cruising any time he wants to, or even becoming brother-like roommates who have sex only with outsiders.

If these new arrangements solved the problem, they'd keep gay marriages together. But it doesn't seem to work that way. The open arrangements work for a while—and then the marriages usually fall apart; as nearly as anyone can tell, open gay marriages have no better chance of lasting than faithful ones—and possibly much less chance. Which oughtn't surprise us, for in gay love, as in heterosexual love, sexual feelings and affection are very closely interwoven. When partners have sex outside the marriage, it unweaves the fabric of love and weakens the feeling of closeness, one-ness, and we-ness between them. Worst of all, it destroys trust: neither partner can ever be sure that the other won't fall in love with someone who was supposed to be only a one-night stand. Infidelity creates fear, and fear creates anger—and love turns into hate.

So even though there is much more infidelity among married gays than among married heterosexuals, and even though most gays say infidelity is "realistic" and necessary, it doesn't work out well for most of them in the long run, any more than it does for heterosexual couples.

Straightening out

Some straight gays are that way from the beginning. More often, straight gays start out looking and acting "queer," but slowly change as they grow older. They gradually give up camping, swishing, or acting superbutch; they drop out of the bar and bath and tearoom marketplace; they start trying to have closer, longerlasting relationships with other gays; and they turn more of their attention to work and to finding ways to adjust to and succeed in the straight world. Some try to "pass" as heterosexuals, hiding every trace of their former gay mannerisms. Others live openly as gays, keeping a certain amount of the manner and style of gayness but basically adopting a straight lifestyle, even as people from another country keep some of their own favorite customs while becoming Americans.

Most straight gays, in short, are that way because they've tried other kinds of homosexual life and found them disappointing or unsatisfying. This isn't the only route to straight homosexuality, however; a more direct one exists, and will become more widely used as the pressures against gays diminish. Dr. Thomas Waddell, a San Francisco physician and a partner in a gay marriage, told *People* magazine not long ago: "There are lots of gays who have stable relationships and simply do not go through the great traumas, the anonymous promiscuity, the one-night stands you always hear about."[168]

But he is speaking more of the future than the present; it is still true today that most straight gays have traveled a long and rocky road to get where they are. Here is a reasonably typical example—here is the life story of one man who tried various kinds of gay life before becoming, eventually, a straight gay. He's a real person, so to protect his privacy I'll change his name and a few minor details; other than that, everything in his story is true just as it is set down here.

James Keiller wouldn't strike you as gay if you saw him on the street. He's a tall, broad-shouldered man of fifty-three, well-built, and with a quick springy step. He combs his sandy-colored hair sideways across the top of his head to hide his bald spot. He likes sports clothes that have flair and style—not swishy, but certainly not ordinary and conventional. He has a big, sunny smile, and his face is manly and strong-jawed, but if you talked to him for a while at a party, you might sense that he was gay. That's because he sometimes says things with a certain gay stress ("Wasn't 'Mary Hartman' just *marvelous* last night? Didn't you a*dore* it?"), and because he sometimes uses campy faces or gestures for fun.

These things aren't accidental slips. Jim Keiller isn't hiding anything; he's been out of the closet for years. He's a straight gay who allows himself to be natural and at ease, without pretending to be something he isn't. He speaks openly about his gayness to close heterosexual friends, and even sometimes mentions it casually when talking to heterosexual business contacts, just as one of them might casually mention his own wife or children.

Jim Keiller was born and grew up in San Diego, California. His father, who wanted to be an architect, couldn't afford to go to college, and became a carpenter and, later, a small-time house builder. Jim's mother, a prim, fussy little woman, spent all her time making her house—and her baby son—as beautiful as possible. Jim was an only child, and because he was blond and cute, his mother dreamed of his becoming a child movie star and kept him at home dressed all in white long after the other boys were out climbing trees and playing touch football. Naturally, he was called "sissy" by most of the neighborhood boys and thought of himself as one; fortunately, he was always taller than most boys his age, and a couple of times, when he was picked on too much and too long, he fought and won his fights. But the other boys thought he had won out of sheer crazy anger; they still considered him a sissy.

That passed; when he was twelve or thirteen and big and strong for his age, his schoolmates more or less forgot about the sissy phase. At that point, Jim himself had no inkling that he was different from the other boys. "I never gave it a thought. When I was twelve or thirteen, we'd goose each other and grope each other in the locker room, and it would get me terribly excited sexually—and still I didn't wonder about myself. When I began to masturbate, instead of thinking about naked women, I'd think about my boy friends in the locker room—but even *that* didn't give me the clue to the truth."

In his teens, Jim was taller and better-looking than most of his classmates, and reasonably popular with both boys and girls. Unaware of his real desires, he pursued the best-looking boy in his class and made a special friend of him, but at the same time, he started dating girls and trying to "make out." "I was known as 'fresh and fast' —I talked fresh, and was fast with my hands. But somehow I could never get anywhere beyond a little feeling and touching. All through high school, when other guys claimed they were 'making it' with one girl or another, I was still a virgin. I felt really ashamed of myself. Sometimes I would date girls who were said to be hot stuff, hoping they'd seduce me, but nothing ever happened. I told myself that the reason I didn't try harder was that I was afraid of being rejected, but the truth probably is that I didn't really want anything to happen."

For a while, Jim solved the problem by going steady with a beautiful girl who was sexually very reserved and refused to let him make any advances, but who was romantic and poetic and loved the idea of their being in love. They danced, they read poetry, they looked at the moon, they kissed tenderly—and neither ever mentioned that there was no physical desire between them. "I was half aware of the fact that neither she nor any other girl excited me sexually, while good-looking boys and male movie stars did. I knew there was something *different* about me. But I told myself I was being saved for something special, some ideal girl, and hadn't met her yet."

At the end of his high-school years, he got the first clear signal. His best friend was about to go off to college, and he and Jim, knowing they wouldn't see each other for a long while, spent a last evening together. "It was a dramatic farewell scene—deep talk and poetry, out under the stars. No touching, of course, but tears, promises, and a pounding heart. And when I went home and thought about it, I said to myself suddenly, 'I'm a fairy! I'm a damn fairy!' "

But the moment of understanding didn't last. Within a few days he told himself that it had been just a passing mood, that he had been going through a phase, and that he wasn't really a fairy, because he hadn't ever done anything fairies do.

Not having money enough for college, Jim moved to Hollywood and got a job as a carpenter, building sets on a movie lot (he'd learned skilled carpentry from his father). In the sexually free atmosphere of Hollywood he met many gay men, and had to admit to himself that in their presence he often felt sexually aroused and wanted to try a homosexual experience. One night, walking home from a heavy necking date with a girl, he let a gay man pick him up, buy him a drink, and take him into a park. The man could tell that Jim was a beginner, and very gently asked if he could perform fellatio on him. "I nodded, and he did, but I was so nervous and frightened and guilty that I hardly felt a thing. Afterward I told myself that I hadn't enjoyed it, and I hadn't *done* anything, so I wasn't really a homosexual, after all.

"That's the way it went for a couple of years. I'd let guys pick me up, talk me into it, and perform on me, but I wouldn't repay the favor, because as long as I didn't *do* anything, I wasn't being homosexual. But little by little I began to like it more, and feel excited about the guys, and I went out less and less with girls, and did so only to keep up appearances when old friends were in town with their wives and wanted to meet me for dinner."

One night, the first time Jim ever went to a gay bar, he met Arnold G., a well-to-do, middle-aged businessman who told Jim he'd "set him up" if Jim would do him a certain favor. Arnold said he'd rent a suite for Jim every weekend at the Beverly Hills Hotel, give Jim credit cards for the local gay clubs, and pay him a salary; all Jim had to do in return was bring home a beautiful gay man each weekend night and let Arnold watch while Jim and the other man had sex. "If anyone had told me I was pimping and prostituting myself, I would have died of shame. It never occurred to me that that was what I was doing. I liked it because I felt *wanted*—by Arnold and by the guys I brought home. Girls had never wanted me the way these men did, and it was terrific for my ego. I thought it was great."

When Jim got his draft call—it was 1944—he told his draft board that he was homosexual and was reclassified 4-F. Just about that time, Arnold lost interest in their arrangement, but by now Jim was an old hand at the gay bar scene and was glad to be free.

For a while he cruised regularly, never spending more than one night with any partner. Then in a bar he met a salesman named Kenneth van W. who developed a crush on him and pursued him, and after a few nights asked Jim to live with him. "I was ready to try it. I didn't have any special feeling about him, but the sex was great, and he was an amusing companion. He thought of us as a couple and I did like him, but I cheated on him like crazy. He was on the road a lot, and the minute he left town I'd head for the bars and do one-night stands or even quickies in the washroom. Ken had taught me to enjoy being sexually active, so I was into all kinds of sex by now and liked them all. But what I really was after was having good-looking men want me and pursue me; what I liked was the feeling of conquest. I never wanted to see any of the guys a second time—I always wanted new ones. I realized that there was something very empty about all this and about my relationship with Ken, but I figured it was my fault. I thought there was something missing in me—I thought I just wasn't capable of loving anyone."

After two years, Jim became bored with Ken and with life in Los Angeles. One day, following a big fight with Ken, he packed up, quit his job, and headed for New York, to make a fresh start. Because of the postwar building boom, he had no trouble finding work with a builder; at the same time, he began going to night school and studying architecture—his father's dream, which Jim was now going to make come true. He lived alone in a rented room, went to school four nights a week, and for social life and sex made the rounds of the gay bars the other three nights.

Then he met a somewhat older man in class and drifted into a relationship with him. "Stanley and I started out as a weekend fling, but we both wanted to keep seeing each other. It was really rather strong—I was surprised, and pleased that I could feel so much—and if it wasn't love, I didn't know the difference. After a few weekends, we moved in together and became a couple. We had a very strong thing going for about a year, and were faithful all that time, but then we both started getting the itch for adventure and new conquests. At first we agreed to do it together. He'd cruise the bars —he was terribly handsome—and he'd snag some guy and bring him home, and we'd have a threesome. But it almost always ended up a mess, because I was sexually much better than he, so it was always competitive and ugly, and afterward we'd have terrible fights.

"After a couple of years of this, we hardly talked to each other any more, and stopped being lovers. We continued to live in the same apartment, but had separate bedrooms, and rarely even ate together. I hardly saw him, anyway—I was in school four nights a week, and at the baths the other three. I had come to dislike the bars, with all the phony acting and talk, and I thought the baths were much more honest. I had no friends and no social life, and all I wanted to do in my spare time was see how many men I could have in one evening. If you're on the receiving end, you can have quite a few—my usual score was twenty or so. When I'd had enough, I'd pick one, and play the active part and get off, and then go home."

In 1953, when he was nearly thirty, Jim got his degree and decided to move to San Francisco, which was becoming the favorite city of gays. He and Stanley, who had been lovers for three years and roommates for three more, parted with hardly a word. In San Francisco, Jim got a job with a large architectural firm, and slowly worked his way up, becoming reasonably successful as a designer of middle-priced modern houses in the suburbs. For some years he lived as a closet gay: he told his business associates that he was divorced, and hinted that he was having an affair with a married woman. Actually, he cruised the gay bars and baths, and from time to time had someone live with him until they tired of each other or had a falling out. Time passed. He was in his mid-thirties, still good-looking but getting a bit beyond the best age for the cruising scene—and feeling, increasingly, that life was empty and pointless.

One day, while working on the design of a new house, he found he needed to come to a decision about certain draperies and wall fabrics, and phoned an interior decorator he had sometimes done business with. The decorator said he'd like to send over Wallace Davis, a new assistant who was highly gifted. A little while later, into Jim's office walked a slim, very handsome young man—obviously gay (at least to Jim's knowing eye), a trifle swish (but only a trifle), and definitely not a queen; in fact, his whole manner was rather reserved and proper. "We started talking business, and in a few minutes I looked deep into Wallie's eyes and knew that this was something new and different for me. Something about him *rang* inside me. He knew perfectly well that I wasn't keeping my mind on business, but he wasn't playing up to me. He was being very careful—he'd just had a bad breakup with a lover, I later found out, and he was still hurting. But before he left, I told him I had to see him and wanted to take him to dinner, and he accepted.

"We talked a blue streak that night; we tried to tell each other everything, all at once. I started talking about sex, and told him that my usual thing was that I went to bed with somebody new the first night and then never saw him again, and before I could say another word he said, 'Well, that's *not* going to be me.' He wasn't having any; I couldn't get near him. But I tried—oh, Lord, I tried, that night, and every night for weeks.

"I really *courted* Wallie—phoned him day and night, sent him gifts, took him places, talked my head off. I found out that he was a very Victorian sort of guy, very pure and untarnished. And I liked that *so* much. I liked the fact that he was so reserved on the surface, but actually full of fun and excitement. We walked in the park, we had dinner, we went to concerts, we talked and talked.

"And then his firm sent him to Seattle for a month. That did it. The weekend before he had to leave, we finally went to bed together. And as soon as it happened, we started using the word 'love'—both of us, at the same time. We had really known it for a while, but now we weren't afraid to say it. And we agreed to be faithful while he was away (neither of us, of course, had been with anyone else sexually since the day we met)—and I found myself excited by the thought of being faithful to someone. I, who used to take on fifty or sixty different guys a week!"

Jim has often asked himself what made him respond to Wallie so differently from the way he had to other men. "I guess I had been growing up slowly, and finally was ready for a real relationship. The other life had long seemed empty and boring. And Wallie was so beautiful, physically and spiritually—so decent, so giving. With other gays, I had always been a bit cruel, a bit of an exploiter, but I wanted to do things for Wallie, wanted to make him happy. And the most important thing, I think, is that he was the first person I ever really trusted —and I felt he could trust me just as much."

Jim flew to Seattle to see Wallie every weekend during their month of separation. Then, as soon as Wallie returned, they went looking for an apartment, found and decorated one, and moved in. That was seventeen years ago; ever since, they have been inseparable, and faithful. "The abstinence from outside sex is an investment in the relationship," Jim says. "Most of the gay couples we know either cheat secretly or have arrangements—and almost always it does something awful to their feelings for each other. I admit that some of them do seem to make it work, but they don't have the kind of closeness and warmth that we have."

These days, Jim and Wallie live in a charming modern house in Sausalito; Jim designed it and Wallie decorated it. They drive to work in San Francisco every morning; it's only fifteen minutes away. Half a dozen years ago, Jim began letting his business partners know that he lived with another man. No one seemed surprised, much less bothered by the news. Jim and Wallie have many gay friends, almost all of them couples, but they avoid most gay parties because there's usually a good deal of cruising going on. For the same reason, they have no interest in going to gay bars, except for one where dancing is more the order of business than cruising. In recent years, as the social disapproval of homosexuality has decreased—especially in San Francisco—they have found themselves socializing easily with married heterosexual couples, and nowadays spend as much time with them as with gay couples.

Both Jim and Wallie earn decent professional incomes. Neither is the "husband" where moneymaking is concerned; they have their own bank accounts, but they share all expenses and co-own their house and their cars. Wallie is good at sewing and needlepoint, but Jim enjoys cooking and does most of it. Jim, who is the taller, older, and more rugged-looking, is the one who makes their social dates—the wife's role in traditional heterosexual marriage. Wallie, on the other hand, though more refined-looking and rather shy compared to Jim, is the hard-headed businessman of the two, and makes most of the decisions about their bigger expenses and investments. When they fight, as they occasionally do, Wallie is the fiercer fighter, Jim the more wounded and slower to get over it. Sexually, they have no fixed or traditional pattern; like many modern husbands and wives, they take turns, each sometimes starting things, each sometimes the more active one and at other times the more passive one.

Thus, while they are two men, and distinctly gay men,

they are very much like straight men and women in many ways, and their relationship is very much like that of a straight husband and wife of the modern, liberated kind. And this is why they can be so close to their heterosexual friends, and why the heterosexual couples they are friends with feel the same kind of respect for Jim and Wallie's relationship that they do for heterosexual marriage.

One such heterosexual couple came to have Thanksgiving dinner with Jim and Wallie this past fall. It was a fine meal, with lots of good wine and good talk and good music. Everyone was feeling wonderfully warm and affectionate when it was time to go, and as the husband and wife were leaving, each of them quite naturally and spontaneously hugged Jim and Wallie. In their car, driving home, the couple talked about it, and the husband said he hadn't felt at all awkward or strange about hugging each of their hosts. His wife said she was glad, and then added, "I hoped so—especially when Wallie kissed you on the mouth."

Her husband looked at her, astonished. "He did?" he asked. Then, after thinking a moment, he added, "I'll be darned—you're right. I never gave it a second thought."

And that's how it may come to be, between straights and gays, some day—perhaps even in your time.

NOTES ON

SOURCES

Page numbers within the named source are not given here if the material can easily be found in that source by means of its index or table of contents.

1. Paul H. Gebhard et al., *Sex Offenders* (New York: Harper & Row and Paul B. Hoeber, Inc., 1965), pp. 642–3, as to gay men. As to lesbians: Isadore Rubin, "Homosexuality," SIECUS Discussion Guide No. 2 (New York: Sex Information and Education Council, 1965).
2. These figures are only approximate; the surveys differ somewhat. They are: Martin S. Weinberg and Colin J. Williams, *Male Homosexuals* (New York: Oxford University Press, 1974); Marcel T. Saghir and Eli Robins, *Male and Female Homosexuality* (Baltimore: Williams & Wilkins, 1973); and Gundlach and Riess, cited in Bettie Wysor, *The Lesbian Myth* (New York: Random House, 1974).

3. Alfred C. Kinsey et al., *Sexual Behavior in the Human Male* (Philadelphia and London: W. B. Saunders, 1948); *Sexual Behavior in the Human Female* (same, 1953).

4. Kinsey (1948) (see note 3).

5. Kinsey (1953) (see note 3).

6. Weinberg and Williams (see note 2); Alan P. Bell, "Homosexualities: Their Range and Character," in James K. Cole and Richard Dienstbier, *Nebraska Symposium on Motivation, 1973* (Lincoln: University of Nebraska Press, 1974).

7. Bell (see note 6); Jack H. Hedblom, "Dimensions of Lesbian Sexual Experience," *Archives of Sexual Behavior*, v. 2, no. 4 (1973), pp. 329–41.

8. Kinsey (1948) and (1953) (see note 3); David Sonenschein, "Are Homosexuals Really Oversexed?" *Sexology*, v. 38 (October 1971).

9. Gebhard et al. (see note 1); Martin Hoffman, *The Gay World* (New York: Basic Books, 1968).

10. Morton Hunt, *Sexual Behavior in the 1970s* (New York: Playboy Press, 1974).

11. Judd Marmor, in John M. Livingood, ed., *Final Report of the National Institute of Mental Health Task Force on Homosexuality* (Rockville, Maryland: National Institute of Mental Health, 1972) (DHEW Publication No. HMS 72–9116).

12. Hunt (see note 10), chapters 3 and 4.

13. Laud Humphries, paper delivered at conference of International Academy of Sex Research held at State University of New York, Stony Brook, September 1975; reported in *The New York Times*, September 17, 1975.

14. Bell (see note 6).

15. Eugene E. Levitt and Albert D. Klassen, "Public Attitudes toward Homosexuality," *Journal of Homosexuality,* v. 1, no. 1 (1974).

16. Edwin M. Schur in Livingood (see note 11); Hedblom (see note 7).

17. C. A. Tripp, *The Homosexual Matrix* (New York: McGraw-Hill Book Co., 1975).

18. Levitt and Klassen (see note 15).

19. Robert Liebert, in Hendrik M. Ruitenbeek, ed., *Homosexuality: A Changing Picture* (London: Souvenir Press, 1973).

20. Gary Alinder, "My Gay Soul," in Karla Jay and Allen Young, eds., *Out of the Closets* (New York: Pyramid, 1972). Ellipses not indicated.

21. Levitt and Klassen (see note 15).

22. No such entries appear, for instance, in the massive bibliography by Martin S. Weinberg and Alan P. Bell, *Homosexuality: An Annotated Bibliography* (New York: Harper & Row, 1972).

23. Donald Clemmer, Alfred C. Kinsey, Robert Lindner, and others cited in Arno Karlen, *Sexuality and Homosexuality* (New York: W. W. Norton & Co., 1971), pp. 552–6.

24. John Money and Anke A. Ehrhardt, *Man & Woman, Boy & Girl* (Baltimore: Johns Hopkins University Press, 1972).

25. Franz J. Kallmann, "Comparative Twin Study on the Genetic Aspects of Male Homosexuality," *Journal of Nervous and Mental Disease,* v. 115, no. 4 (1952), pp. 283–98.

26. Money, in Livingood (see note 11).

27. Money, in Livingood (see note 11); W. J. Gadpaille,

"Innate Masculine-Feminine Differences," *Medical Aspects of Human Sexuality*, February 1973.

28. Same as note 27.

29. Robert C. Kolodny et al., "Plasma Testosterone and Semen Analysis in Male Homosexuals," *New England Journal of Medicine*, v. 285 (November 18, 1971), pp. 1170–4.

30. For this statement and the following case, see Money and Ehrhardt (note 24), pp. 154–60.

31. David H. Rosen, *Lesbianism* (Springfield: Charles C. Thomas, 1974), pp. 55–6.

32. Sigmund Freud, letter to an American mother, April 9, 1935, in Ernest Jones, *The Life and Work of Sigmund Freud* (New York: Basic Books, 1957), v. 3, p. 195.

33. Same as note 11.

34. Irving Bieber et al., *Homosexuality: A Psychoanalytic Study* (New York: Basic Books, 1962).

35. Evelyn Hooker, "The Adjustment of the Male Overt Homosexual," [1957], in Hendrik M. Ruitenbeek, ed., *The Problem of Homosexuality in Modern America* (New York: E. P. Dutton & Co., 1963).

36. Same as note 11.

37. See, for instance, Hoffman (note 9); Saghir and Robins (note 2); Hedblom (note 7); and Martin Manosevitz, "The Development of Male Homosexuality," *Journal of Sex Research*, v. 8, no. 1 (1972).

38. Bell (see note 6).

39. Clellan S. Ford and Frank A. Beach, *Patterns of Sexual Behavior* (New York: Harper & Brothers and Paul B. Hoeber, Inc., 1951).

40. For résumés of the evidence, see Hunt (note 10), p. 299, and Karlen (note 23), pp. 399–402.

41. On the whole paragraph: same sources as in note 40, plus note 39.

42. Levitt and Klassen (see note 15).

43. Weinberg and Williams (see note 2); "American Laws Applicable to Consensual Adult Homosexual Acts," direct communication to Morton Hunt from the American Civil Liberties Union, November 1975.

44. Same as note 43.

45. *The New York Times*, May 26, 1975, p. 1; *Time*, September 8, 1975, p. 36.

46. E. Carrington Boggan et al., *The Rights of Gay People* [an American Civil Liberties Union handbook] (New York: Avon Books, 1975).

47. Gebhard, cited in Livingood (see note 11), p. 7.

48. Same as note 46.

49. Weinberg and Williams (see note 2), p. 108; Dr. George Weinberg, in preface to Lige Clark and Jack Nichols, *Roommates Can't Always Be Lovers* (New York: St. Martin's Press, 1974).

50. Gebhard, cited in Livingood (see note 11), p. 7.

51. Weinberg and Williams (see note 2), pp. 116–17.

52. On the history of repression of homosexuality from early Christian era: Katz, in Livingood (see note 11); Karlen (see note 23), p. 78; and Havelock Ellis, *Sexual Inversion* (originally published in German in 1896), pp. 346–50, in his *Studies in the Psychology of Sex*, v. 1 (New York: Random House [1936]).

53. On this whole paragraph: same as note 52, but for Karlen, pp. 190–6.

54. Kinsey (1948) and (1953) (see note 3).

55. Bieber et al. (see note 34), p. 276.

56. Weinberg and Williams (see note 2), pp. 19–20.

57. Levitt and Klassen (see note 15).

58. Martha Shelley, "Gay Is Good," in Jay and Young (see note 20).

59. Peter Wyden and Barbara Wyden, *Growing Up Straight* (New York: Stein & Day, 1968), p. 32.

60. For the brief history of gay liberation in the next six paragraphs, I have drawn on many accounts; the briefest and most impartial is contained in Weinberg and Williams (see note 2), pp. 27–38. See also Donald J. Cantor, in Lester A. Kirkendall and Robert N. Whitehurst, eds., *The New Sexual Revolution* (New York: Donald W. Brown, Inc., 1971).

61. *The New York Times*, July 10, 1975, p. 8; and for the latest number of cities, letter from Bruce Voeller, executive director of the National Gay Task Force, in *The New York Times Magazine*, December 21, 1975.

62. *The New York Times*, July 10, 1975, p. 8; *Playboy*, "Forum Newsfront," January 1976, p. 44.

63. Weinberg and Williams (see note 2), p. 115.

64. Money says so in "Q & A," *Medical Aspects of Human Sexuality*, November 19, 1975.

65. Herbert Hendin, *The Age of Sensation* (New York: Norton, 1975), pp. 115, 118; letter from Dr. Judd Marmor in *The New York Times*, September 12, 1975.

66. Kinsey (1948) and (1953) (see note 3).

67. Hunt (see note 10).

68. Kinsey (1948) (see note 3), p. 169; Saghir and Robins (see note 2), pp. 52, 54.

69. Kinsey (1953) (see note 3), pp. 466–7, 492.

70. Saghir and Robins (see note 2), p. 222.

71. Kinsey (1948) (see note 3), p. 170; Weinberg and Williams (see note 2), p. 111; Saghir and Robins (see note 2), pp. 53–4.

72. Kinsey (1953) (see note 3), pp. 466–7, 492; Saghir and Robins (see note 2), pp. 221–2.

73. Hunt (see note 10).

74. Hunt (see note 10); Weinberg and Williams (see note 2), p. 111; Saghir and Robins (see note 2), pp. 53–4.

75. Hunt (see note 10); Saghir and Robins (see note 2), p. 222.

76. Ford and Beach (see note 39), pp. 130–4.

77. Hunt (see note 10).

78. Bell (see note 6); Weinberg and Williams (see note 2), pp. 111–12; Saghir and Robins (see note 2), pp. 53–4.

79. Karlen (see note 23), p. 196.

80. Hunt (see note 10); Saghir and Robins (see note 2), p. 220.

81. Same as note 80; also, S/M is not even mentioned in Weinberg and Williams (see note 2), Hoffman (see note 9), etc. Tripp (see note 17) suggests that 1 to 2 percent of gay men are involved in S/M.

82. As in note 81, none of the major up-to-date sources even mentions it.

83. Saghir and Robins (see note 2), p. 82.

84. Saghir and Robins (see note 2) say none does (p. 241), but some lesbians claim to do so. See, for instance, Jill Johnston, *Lesbian Nation: The Feminist Solution* (New York: Simon and Schuster, 1973).

85. Sandy Boucher, "Mountain Radio," *Ms.* magazine, April

1975. Ellipses not indicated; tenses of verbs changed in second sentence.

86. Saghir and Robins (see note 2), pp. 59–60, 230–1; Hoffman (see note 9), pp. 13–17, 141.

87. First two sentences: Mark Freedman, *Homosexuality and Psychological Functioning* (Belmont, Calif.: Brooks/Cole, 1971), p. 51; rest of quote: same author, "Homosexuals May Be Healthier than Straights," *Psychology Today*, March 1975.

88. Johnston (see note 84), p. 187; ellipses not indicated.

89. Laud Humphreys, "Tearoom Trade," *Trans-Action*, January 1970.

90. Bell (see note 6).

91. Weinberg and Williams (see note 2), pp. 111–12, compared to heterosexual frequencies reported in Hunt (see note 10), p. 190; Saghir and Robins (see note 2); and homosexual frequencies reported in Hunt, pp. 315–16. Kinsey (1948) and (1953) (see note 3) had reported low frequencies for homosexuals in the 1940's.

92. Saghir and Robins (see note 2), pp. 18–19, 193–4.

93. Judd Marmor, in Livingood (see note 11); Kurt Freund et al., "Measuring Feminine Gender Identity in Homosexual Males," *Archives of Sexual Behavior*, v. 3, no. 3 (1974), pp. 249–60.

94. Wysor (see note 2), pp. 141–2.

95. See discussion of the Terman M–F tests in Morton Hunt, *Her Infinite Variety* (New York: Harper & Row, 1962).

96. For one easily available discussion of labeling, see Donald Light, Jr., and Suzanne Keller, *Sociology* (New York: Alfred A. Knopf, 1975).

97. Saghir and Robins (see note 2), pp. 20–1; ellipses not indicated; some punctuation added.

98. Hunt (see note 10), pp. 322–3; Karlen (see note 23), pp. 399–402.

99. James Elias and Paul Gebhard, "Sexuality and Sexual Learning in Childhood," *Phi Delta Kappan*, March 1969; Manosevitz (see note 37); Hunt (see note 10), p. 317.

100. Elias and Gebhard (see note 99); Gebhard, in Livingood (see note 11); Hunt (see note 10), p. 317.

101. Hunt (see note 10), pp. 322–3; ellipses not indicated.

102. Saghir and Robins (see note 2), pp. 39, 61.

103. Saghir and Robins (see note 2), pp. 88–90; Bell (see note 6).

104. Same as note 103.

105. Hedblom (see note 7); Gebhard, in Livingood (see note 11); Saghir and Robins (see note 2), pp. 205–6, 213.

106. Hedblom (see note 7); Saghir and Robins (see note 2), pp. 247–8.

107. Saghir and Robins (see note 2), pp. 84–6.

108. Tripp (see note 17), p. 137.

109. Howard J. Brown, in *Medical World News*, October 26, 1973, p. 18.

110. Percentages from Kinsey (1948) and (1953), applied to 1974 totals of married men and women from *Statistical Abstract of the United States, 1974* (Washington: U.S. Bureau of the Census, 1974).

111. Barry M. Dank, "Coming Out in the Gay World," *Psychiatry*, v. 34 (May 1971); and for females, same sources as in note 105.

112. Dank (see note 111).

113. Carol A. B. Warren, *Identity and Community in the Gay World* (New York: John Wiley & Sons, 1974), p. 161; ellipses not indicated.

114. Wysor (see note 2).

115. Dank (see note 111).

116. Sue Kiefer Hammersmith and Martin S. Weinberg, "Homosexual Identity: Commitment, Adjustment, and Significant Others," *Sociometry*, v. 36, no. 1 (1973), pp. 56–79.

117. Saghir and Robins (see note 2), pp. 127, 286.

118. Hoffman (see note 9), p. 126; Gebhard, cited in Edward Sagarin, "The High Personal Cost of Wearing a Label," *Psychology Today*, March 1976.

119. Dr. Charles Silverstein, quoted in AP story of April 12, 1975; Ruitenbeek, in Ruitenbeek (see note 19), p. 203.

120. Tripp (see note 17), pp. 94–6.

121. Hoffman (see note 9), pp. 29–30; Humphreys (see note 89).

122. *Time*, May 13, 1974, p. 79.

123. Warren (see note 113); Ellis (see note 52), pp. 26–7, 32–3, 294–6.

124. George Domino, "Homosexuality and Creativity," paper presented at 1973 American Psychological Association convention, Montreal.

125. Domino (see note 124); Karlen (see note 23), p. 515; Bell (see note 6).

126. Hooker, in Livingood (see note 11).

127. Weinberg and Williams (see note 2), p. 21.

128. Weinberg and Williams (see note 2), p. 114.

129. Weinberg and Williams (see note 2), p. 115.

130. Weinberg and Williams (see note 2), p. 117.

131. Saghir and Robins (see note 2), p. 240.

132. Warren (see note 113), pp. 82–3, 131.

133. Weinberg and Williams (see note 2), pp. 114–15, 117.

134. Dennis Altman, *Homosexual: Oppression and Liberation* (New York: Avon Books, 1971), p. 62.

135. Allen Young, "Rapping with a Street Transvestite Revolutionary," in Jay and Young (see note 20); ellipses not indicated.

136. Peter Fisher, *The Gay Mystique* (New York: Stein & Day, 1973), pp. 78–9.

137. Money and Ehrhardt (see note 24), p. 244.

138. Money, in Livingood (see note 11); Hoffman (see note 9), pp. 185–6.

139. Warren (see note 113), pp. 132, 135.

140. Warren (see note 113), p. 135.

141. Warren (see note 113), pp. 133, 135.

142. Bell (see note 6).

143. Bell (see note 6); Hoffman (see note 9), p. 165.

144. *Time*, September 8, 1975, pp. 33–4.

145. Hoffman (see note 9), pp. 50–4; *Vector*, July 1975, p. 30.

146. The whole paragraph: Martin S. Weinberg and Colin J. Williams, "The Social Organization of Impersonal Sex: Gay Baths and Other Contexts," paper to appear in *Social Problems*. Written in 1975. Also see Hoffman (note 9), pp. 47–50.

147. Humphreys (see note 89).

148. Konstantin Berlandt, in Jay and Young (see note 20); ellipses not indicated.

149. Weinberg and Williams (see note 2), p. 118.

150. Averages for both gays and straights: Bell (see note 6).

151. Saghir and Robins (see note 2), pp. 223–4, 229.

152. Hoffman (see note 9), throughout, but especially pp. 171–2; Tripp (see note 17), p. 142.

153. Weinberg and Williams (see note 2), p. 113.

154. Saghir and Robins (see note 2), pp. 224–5; William Simon and John H. Gagnon, "The Lesbians: A Preliminary Overview," in John H. Gagnon and William Simon, eds., *Sexual Deviance* (New York: Harper & Row, 1967).

155. Maurice Leznoff and William A. Westley, "The Homosexual Community," in Gagnon and Simon (see note 154).

156. The major sources for the description in this section and the following section of the chapter are: Warren (see note 113); Saghir and Robins (see note 2); and Martin S. Weinberg, "The Male Homosexual," *Social Problems,* v. 17, no. 4 (Spring 1970).

157. Quoted in *Homosexual Counseling Journal,* v. 1, no. 3 (July 1974), p. 118; ellipses not indicated.

158. Boggan et al. (see note 46), pp. 104–7.

159. Weinberg and Williams (see note 2), p. 113.

160. Same as note 157, but p. 91.

161. Bell (see note 6).

162. Simon and Gagnon (see note 154); Saghir and Robins (see note 2), pp. 224–5.

163. Saghir and Robins (see note 2), pp. 72, 236.

164. Tripp (see note 17), p. 169; and Tripp, quoted in *Homosexual Counseling Journal,* v. 1, no. 3 (July 1974), p. 101.

165. Kinsey (1948) and (1953) (see note 3); Hunt (see note 10).

166. Saghir and Robins (see note 2), p. 57.

167. Saghir and Robins (see note 2), pp. 226–7.

168. *People,* October 11, 1976, pp. 51–2.

G L O S S A R Y

This is a list of special terms used by homosexuals, or by straights about homosexuals, that have been mentioned in this book. Because many of them are slang or argot, they are not always used or defined in the same way, but the definitions given here are those which are generally accepted.

active—Having to do with the insertor role in homosexual sex activities

auntie—A middle-aged or elderly male homosexual, especially of an effeminate nature

bisexual—A person more or less equally attracted to both sexes, sexually and emotionally

bitch—In prison slang, a feminine-looking woman who is used sexually, as insertee, by tougher females; also, in gay male slang, a general term of abuse for a nellie or swishy gay male

bull—In prison slang, a tough female who plays the insertor role sexually *bull dyke*—A lesbian who adopts masculine manners and, often, men's clothing

butch—A homosexual male or female who is masculine in looks and manner

camp—Gay male behavior of a deliberately and humorously exaggerated feminine kind; also, art, writing, furnishings, and clothing of a dated, ugly, or vulgar nature, when enjoyed for their absurd or laughable qualities

chicken—A young person, especially a boy, sought and used sexually by an adult homosexual

chickenhawk—An adult homosexual, especially a male, who seeks children or young teen-agers for sexual activities

closet; in the closet—Maintaining secrecy about one's homosexuality

closet gay—A homosexual who hides his or her homosexuality from the world

come out—To recognize, within oneself, that one is a homosexual; also, to make one's first visit to a public place where homosexuals meet, and to become part of that society

cruise—To go looking for a homosexual pickup or sex partner for a brief, instant sex encounter

cunnilingus—The act of kissing a female's sexual parts and stimulating them with the tongue

deviant—As used by gays about other gays: homosexual behavior that is particularly strange or bizarre, e.g., transvestism, child molesting, etc.

diesel dyke—A particularly masculine or tough lesbian

dildo—An artificial penis

dominant—Having to do with the insertor role in homosexual sex activities; the "masculine" or "master" in such sex activities

drag—The clothing of the opposite sex; especially female clothing when worn by a male

drag queen—A gay male who dresses as a woman in a spirit of camp or play-acting; not to be confused with transvestite (which see)

dyke—A lesbian

fag, faggot—A homosexual man, especially an effeminate one

fairy—Same as "fag"

fellatio—The act of kissing and mouthing a sex partner's penis

femme—A feminine-looking lesbian

flaming faggot—A particularly effeminate and flamboyant homosexual man

freak—A deviant of some kind (see *deviant*)

fruit—A gay male, especially an effeminate one

gay—Homosexual, or a homosexual; said of either men or women

girl—In prison slang, a male who is used sexually by other males; an insertee

gorilla—In prison slang, a tough male who plays the insertor role sexually

hustler—A prostitute; in homosexual use, a male prostitute, especially a young male who takes pay to let himself be fellated

insertee—A homosexual man who plays the receptor role in sex, that is, receives the partner's penis orally or anally; a homosexual female who receives the partner's tongue in her sexual parts

insertor—A homosexual man who places his penis in the partner's mouth or anus; a homosexual female who performs cunnilingus on her partner

jock, jocker—A tough or masculine homosexual male; a male insertor

john—The paying customer of a hustler

leather freak—A homosexual, usually male, who dresses in leather and usually acts tough and masculine

lesbian—A female homosexual

marriage, married—In homosexual terms, a homosexual couple who live together, are closely bound by ties of love and sex, and consider themselves a couple

master—The dominant, active, or insertor partner, especially in S/M sex

nellie—An effeminate gay man

nellie queen—An effeminate gay man who is rather extreme and tends to show off; a flaming faggot

one-night stand—A sexual encounter with a stranger that is limited to a single night's acquaintance

oral sex—Fellatio or cunnilingus

out of the closet—Living openly as a homosexual, making no secret of it

pansy—An effeminate gay man

passive—Having to do with the insertee role in homosexual sex

pervert—As used by homosexuals about other homosexuals: a deviant (see *deviant*); a homosexual whose behavior is particularly bizarre or antisocial

piss-elegant—Overly refined, fussy, pretentious

punk—In prison slang, a male who is used sexually by other males; an insertee

queen—A general term, usually scornful, for various kinds of effeminate male homosexuals; often combined with some other word, as in "drag queen," "screaming queen," etc.

queer—A homosexual, especially a male homosexual

queer-baiter—A straight man or youth who, usually traveling in a gang, beats up gay men

queer queers—Deviants (see *deviant*)

quickie—A hasty sex act between strangers

rough trade—Extra-tough, masculine men who claim to be straight but will play the insertor part in homosexual sex

screaming queen—An extremely flamboyant and effeminate homosexual man (same as *flaming faggot*)

S/M (*sadomasochism*)—Sexual relations in which one partner purposely hurts the other physically and both partners become sexually excited by this activity

sodomite—One who performs sodomy, especially a male homosexual

sodomy—(1) Anal intercourse; also, (2) according to the laws of some states, fellatio or cunnilingus

slave—The submissive, passive, or insertee partner, especially in S/M sex

straight—Heterosexual, or a heterosexual

stud—In prison slang, a tough female who plays the insertor role sexually

submissive—Having to do with the insertee role in homosexual sex activities; the "feminine" or "slave" in such activities

swishy—Particularly effeminate; said of a male gay

tearoom—A public place, usually a men's toilet ("t-room" or "tearoom" stands for "toilet room"), where male homosexuals meet for quickie sex, generally fellatio

tearoom trade—Those who take part in sex in tearooms (see *tearoom*)

transsexual—A person, usually male, who undergoes surgery and hormone treatment to change his or her sex

transvestite—A man or woman who not only dresses as someone of the opposite sex but believes, and tries to make others believe, that he or she actually is of the opposite sex

trash—Deviant (see *deviant*)

tricking—Cruising; seeking and having quick sex with strangers

wise—Understanding and tolerant of homosexuality; said of heterosexuals who know about particular homosexuals and are accepting of them

A LIST

FOR FURTHER

READING

———

This is a selected list of recent books dealing with homo-sexuality, for those who want to read further. A word or two follows each listing, telling what particular value that item has.

Boggan, E. Carrington, et al. *The Rights of Gay People.* New York: Avon Books, 1975. An American Civil Liberties Handbook; a review of current laws throughout the United States.

Clarke, Lige, and Jack Nichols. *Roommates Can't Always Be Lovers.* New York: St. Martin's Press, 1974. Letters to *Gay* (a newspaper) and answers by the editors; an inside look at how male gays think and talk.

Fisher, Peter. *The Gay Mystique.* New York: Stein & Day, 1972. A gay man discusses the myths and realities of homo-sexuality today. The emphasis is on male homosexuality; the book is popular rather than scientific, and leans toward gay activist views.

Freedman, Mark. *Homosexuality and Psychological Functioning.* Belmont, California: Brooks/Cole, 1971. A gay psychologist tries to prove that gays are psychologically as healthy as straights, and perhaps even healthier. Science plus exaggeration; interesting, but to be taken with a grain of salt.

Hoffman, Martin. *The Gay World.* New York: Basic Books, 1968; also, Bantam paperback, 1969. A straight psychiatrist portrays the homosexual life in and around San Francisco scientifically, vividly, sympathetically. Respected by straights and gays alike.

Jay, Karla, and Allen Young, eds. *Out of the Closets.* New York: Pyramid Books, 1972. An anthology of writings by gay liberationists, both male and female; angry, propagandistic, and sometimes shocking. One side of the gay experience.

Johnston, Jill. *Lesbian Nation: The Feminist Solution.* New York: Simon and Schuster, 1973. A mostly angry, often very personal discussion of one lesbian's experiences and of the lesbian liberation movement. Highly political and propagandistic.

Karlen, Arno. *Sexuality and Homosexuality: A New View.* New York: W. W. Norton & Company, Inc., 1971. A huge book covering homosexuality historically, legally, and scientifically. Impartial, excellently researched, readable; probably the best all-around book on the subject, although slightly dated now.

Miller, Merle. *On Being Different.* New York: Random House, 1971. A brief, painful, enlightening account of this well-known novelist's many years in the closet, and his coming out; the meaning of homosexuality for a sensitive man—and the changes that have recently come about in that meaning.

Rosen, David H. *Lesbianism*. Springfield: Charles C Thomas, 1974. A brief study by a psychiatrist of twenty-six lesbians; readable case histories and explanations. Takes a liberal position.

Ruitenbeek, Hendrik M., ed. *Homosexuality: A Changing Picture*. London: Souvenir Press Ltd., 1973. An anthology of popular and scientific articles, mostly by straights. Covers a number of interesting topics. Views range from the cautious to the radical.

Saghir, Marcel T., and Eli Robins. *Male and Female Homosexuality*. Baltimore: Williams & Wilkins, 1973. Two psychiatrists report on their recent survey of male and female homosexuals. Difficult reading, heavily scientific and statistical, but valuable and factual.

Tripp, C. A. *The Homosexual Matrix*. New York: McGraw-Hill Book Company, 1975. A psychologist discusses various aspects of homosexuality today; emphasis is on the male side. Often wise and enlightening—but often propagandistic and partial toward gays.

Warren, Carol A. B. *Identity and Community in the Gay World*. New York: John Wiley & Sons, 1974. A sociologist visits and describes gay social life in various parts of California today. Highly readable; not propagandistic.

Weinberg, Martin S., and Colin J. Williams. *Male Homosexuals: Their Problems and Adaptations*. New York: Oxford University Press, 1974. A careful scientific analysis of a recent major survey of male homosexuals by the Institute for Sex Research. Thoroughly liberal but not doctrinaire. Solid factual material and data; invaluable for those who want to understand the topic, and who can deal with technical language and statistics.

Wysor, Bettie. *The Lesbian Myth*. New York: Random House, 1974. A lesbian reviews various beliefs about lesbianism in the light of recent scientific evidence, and interviews a number of lesbians, who speak for themselves.

ABOUT THE AUTHOR

Morton Hunt's first book for young readers was *The Young Person's Guide to Love*. His other books include *The Natural History of Love, The World of the Formerly Married, The Affair*, and *Sexual Behavior in the 1970s*. Mr. Hunt has also written some 300 articles on psychological and sociological subjects for magazines such as *The New Yorker, Harper's, McCall's*, and *The New York Times Magazine*.